CHILDREN'S COGNITIVE ENHANCEMENT PROGRAM YELLOW BOOK:

COMBINED LEVELS
REVISED EDITION

Kenneth Kohutek, Ph.D. & Ann Marie Kohutek, Ed.S.

Illustrated by:

David Orenday & Andrea Izaguirre

© Kenneth Kohutek 2012

ISBN-13: 978-0-9891164-5-9

To learn more about CCEP or to purchase our products, visit kenneth@kennethkohutek.com

Printed in the United States of America

Introduction

This manual is a companion to the *Children's Cognitive Enhancement Program: Combined Levels Revised Edition*. Similar to that manual, it is the combination of the Primary and Elementary levels in one manual. While both the Primary and Elementary manuals serves a specific level of students, this edition is intended for students who might benefit from both, such as those seeking additional training.

 The program originated with students experiencing academic difficulty. However, as it developed and utilized in different settings it became obvious that a large number of students could benefit from completing it. Studies have explored its utility with elementary grades (K-2) as well as in a class of students with learning difficulties. Research on its utility continues in several locations at the time of this writing.

Deficits in the cognitive skills addressed have been found to be predictors of both math and language skills. While there is no "magic" pill or program to "cure" future academic difficulties, there is much research supporting the idea that skills, such as attention, memory and problem-solving can be improved with training.

At first glance, the format may appear deceivingly simple. Upon review of the Introduction and suggestions to the guide, one sees that this program is much more comprehensive. The challenges are a portion but not the entire program. The major emphasis is the relationship between the "guide" and student. The guide provides structure, ideas, and encouragement as the challenges increase in difficulty. Support for this model comes from a wide range of areas and the interested reader is referred to my website for additional information (www.kennethkohutek.com).

This manual is not intended to be just another "brain-based" program that maximizes "neuroplasticity". While both of the concepts are actively being researched, the claims usually are greater than the stastical support. On-going studies on this program have found it to be beneficial in improving memory, planning, inductive reasoning. Research continues to explore strengths and weaknesses as well as drive efforts to improve the program.

The program is not a one-day venture. Rather, it is meant to be used as short (20-30min.) periods occurring once or twice a week. The sessions should be divided between the two manuals equally. It is interesting that some children perform better on tasks in one manual than in the other. In general, this manual is used later in the session. Students appear to enjoy these challenges and going to this manual has been used as a reinforcer for progress in the first manual. It is the guide's responsibility to be responsive to the student's attention and abilities when considering the length or the use of time in a session.

YELLOW BOOK NOTES

Student's Name: _____   Date Started: _____

ITEM   COMMENTS

4	_____	12	_____
5	_____	13	_____
6	_____	14	_____
7	_____	15	_____
8	_____	16	_____
9	_____	17	_____
10	_____	18	_____
11	_____	19	_____
		20	_____

23	_____	33	_____
24	_____	34	_____
25	_____	35	_____
26	_____	36	_____
27	_____	37	_____
28	_____	38	_____
29	_____	39	_____
30	_____	40	_____
31	_____	41	_____
32	_____	42	_____
		43	_____

46	_____	55	_____
47	_____	56	_____
48	_____	57	_____
49	_____	58	_____
50	_____	59	_____
51	_____	60	_____
52	_____	61	_____
53	_____	62	_____
54	_____	63	_____

66	_____	74	_____
67	_____	75	_____
68	_____	76	_____
69	_____	77	_____
70	_____	78	_____
71	_____	79	_____
72	_____	80	_____
73	_____	81	_____

85	____	95	____
86	____	96	____
87	____	97	____
88	____	98	____
89	____	99	____
90	____	100	____
91	____	101	____
92	____	102	____
93	____	103	____
94	____		

106	____	116	____
107	____	117	____
108	____	118	____
109	____	119	____
110	____	120	____
111	____	121	____
112	____	122	____
113	____		
114	____		
115	____		

125	____	135	____
126	____	136	____
127	____	137	____
128	____	138	____
129	____	139	____
130	____	140	____
131	____	141	____
132	____	142	____
133	____	143	____
134	____		

TABLE OF CONTENTS

LEVEL A

TO THE GUIDE

Similar to the first manual **you**, the guide, are an integral part of this journey. That is why you have the title "guide". The actual completion of the levels is the medium to teach the targeted cognitive skills. Necessary skills for completion of these challenges include: attention, memory, planning, visual-spatial and fine motor skills.

Prior to starting any of the challenges the following questions need to be asked:" 1) How many rubber bands do you think you will need to complete this challenge? ; 2) Where are you going to start? Then what? (and so on); 3) Do you think you will be able to complete this design?" These instructions provide a buffer of time allowing the child to think about what is going to happen prior to acting. By encouraging problem-solving skills prior to action, students, regardless of age or ability, are being trained to engage in more effective problem-solving. Also, during the thinking time, the guide is providing structure by demonstrating skills required in the problem-solving process. Through repetition and encouragement the student the likelihood of a transfer of skills increases. Upon completion of the challenge, the guide is encouraged to praise and encourage the student to reflect on how they were able to complete the task. During these reflections, it would be useful to ask if there are other occasions in which such reflection and problem-solving skills would be beneficial.

This is called a geoboard and, using these rubber bands, you can make many different designs on it. Have you ever used one in any of your classes? …

We are going to use this geoboard and these rubber bands to solve the challenges in this book. First you will see challenges on these pages, I will ask you some questions about that challenge while we look for clues, then you can make the design using the rubber bands and geoboard.

Before we get started would you like to make a design of your own for practice?

Here is the first challenge. Before you complete this design, however, I want you to answer some questions. First, how many rubber bands will you need to complete this challenge? ...OK. Next, where are you going to start? ...And then what? Tell me the moves all the way to the finish. Finally, do you think you will be able to complete this design?"

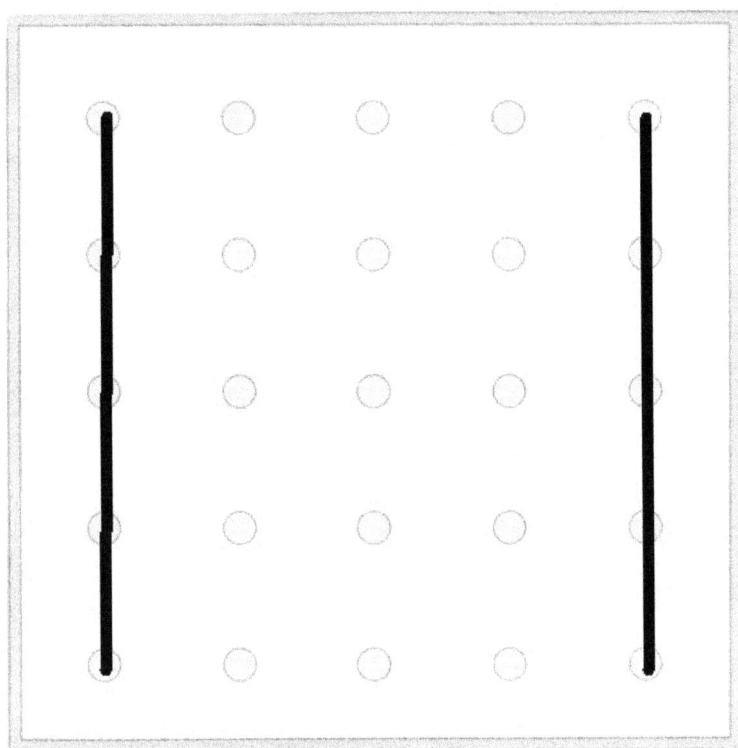

Do the same thing on this page. First, tell me how many rubber bands you will need to complete this challenge? Next, where are you going to start and the steps you will take to finish. Then let me know if you think you will be able to complete the design.

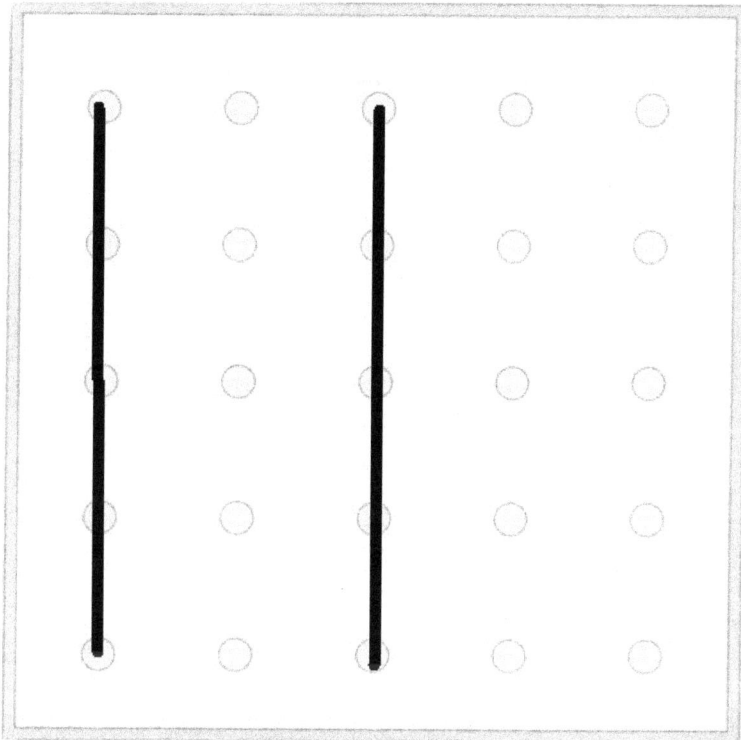

How about this one?

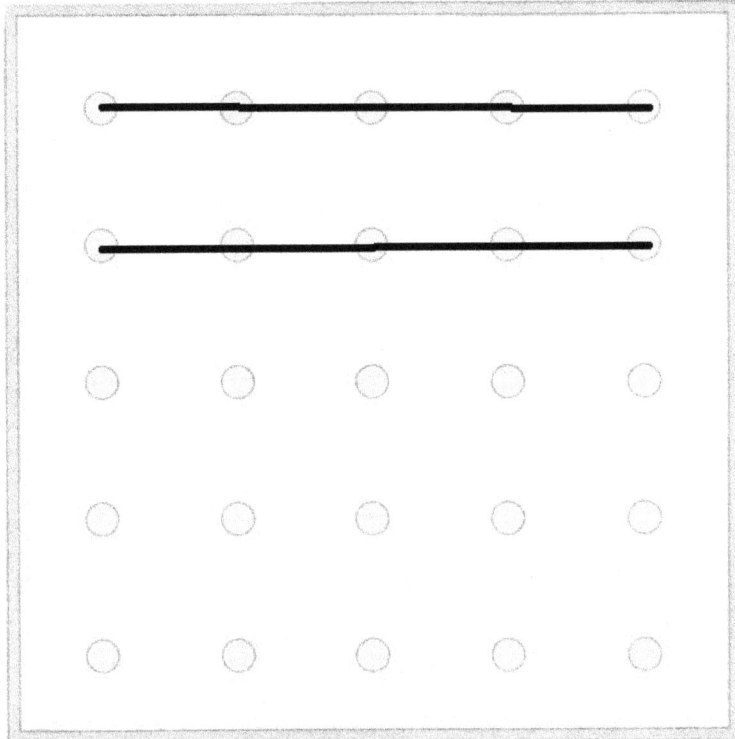

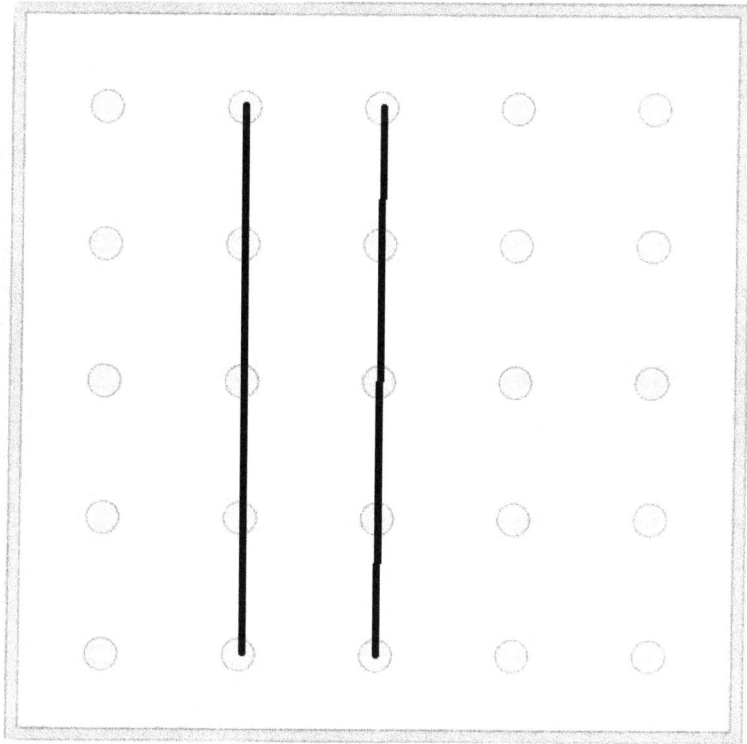

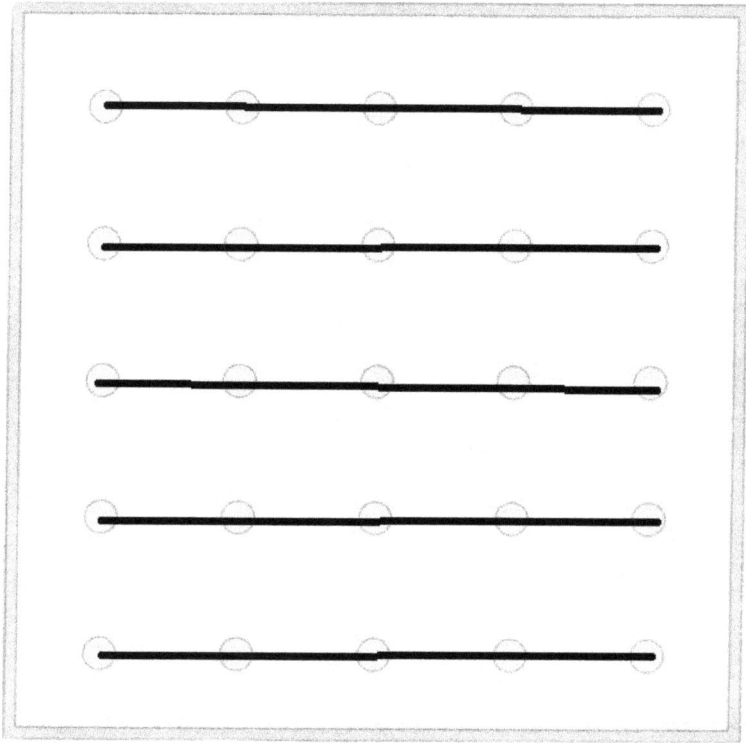

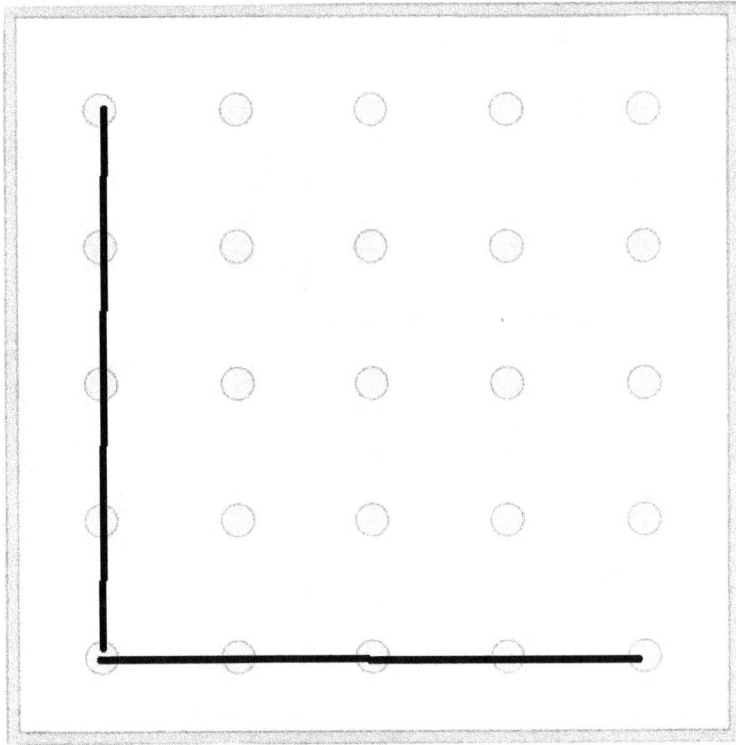

10

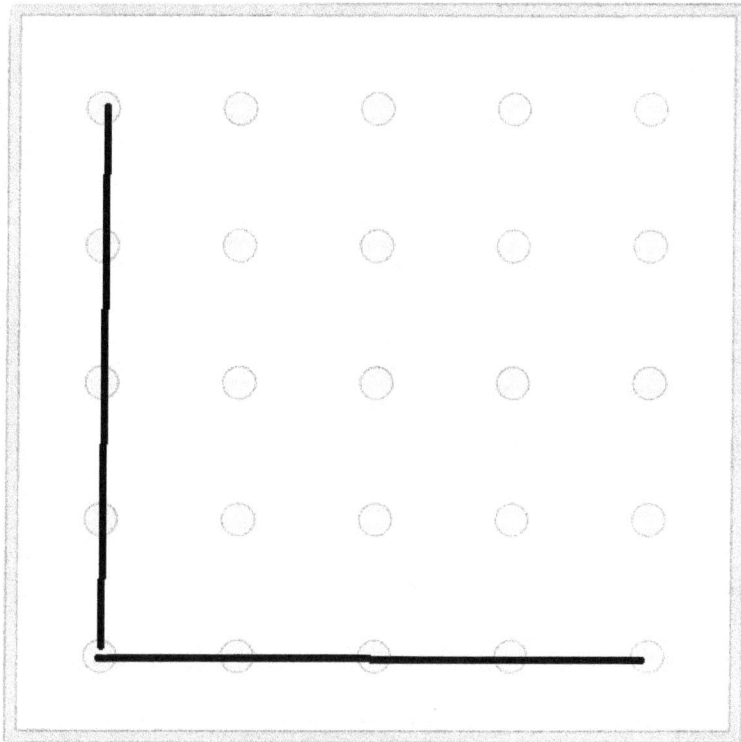

This is the same design. But this time, make the design with one rubber band?
(Skip this page if the previous page was completed with one rubber band.)

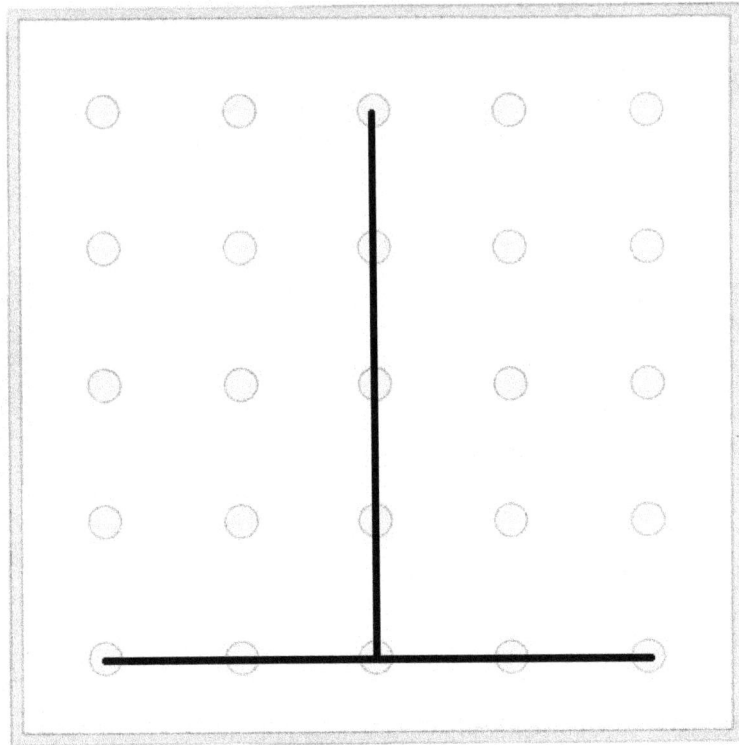

Do this one the same way!

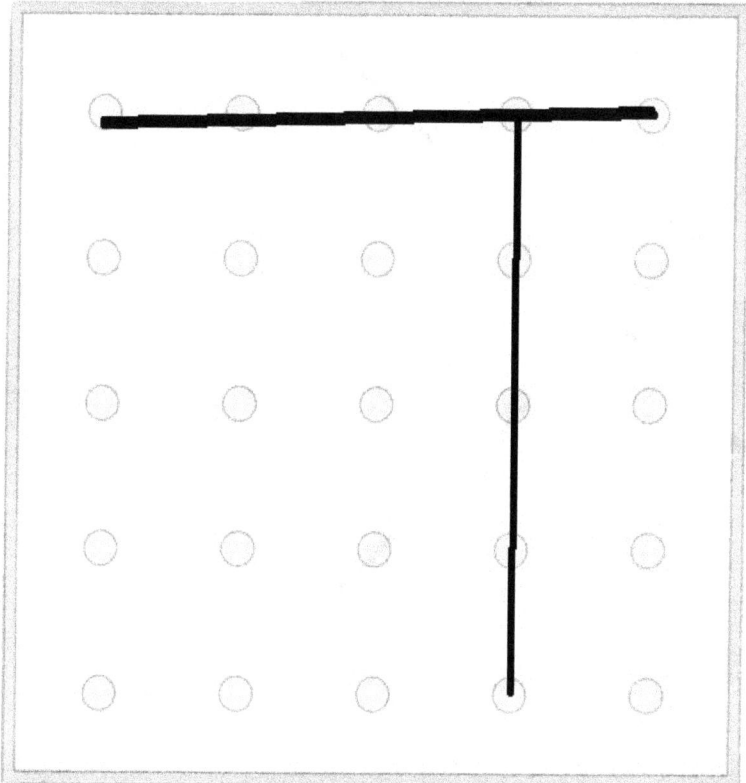

Remember... tell me your plan BEFORE you start
completing the design.

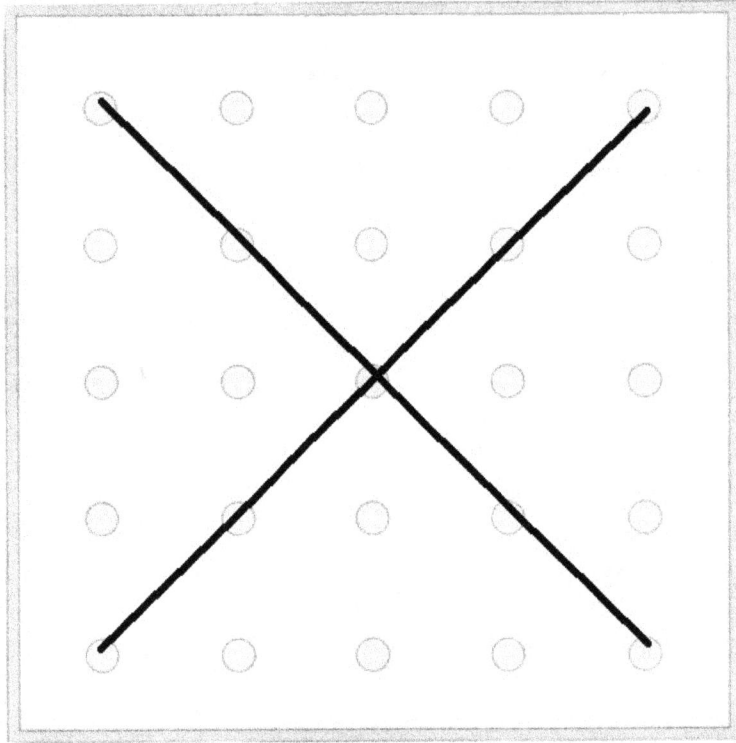

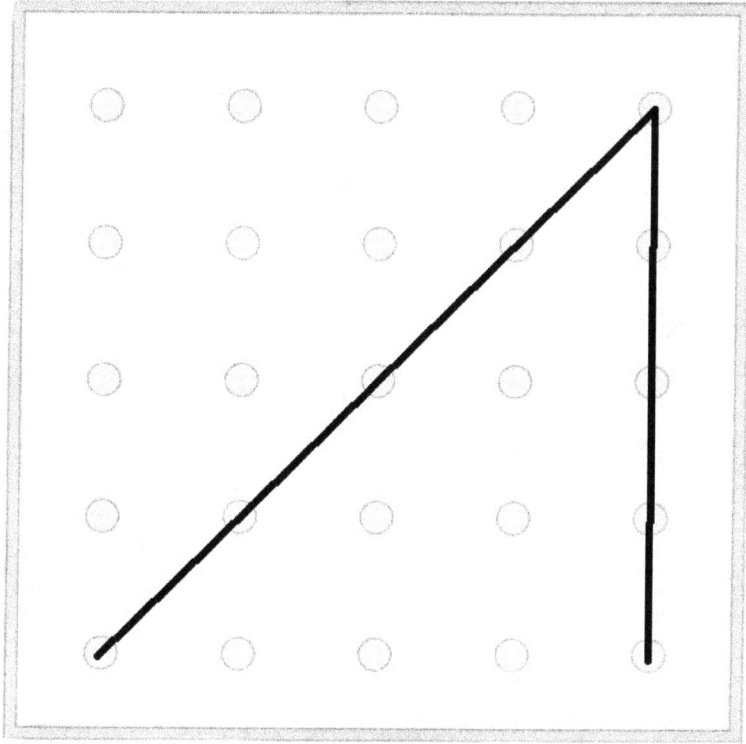

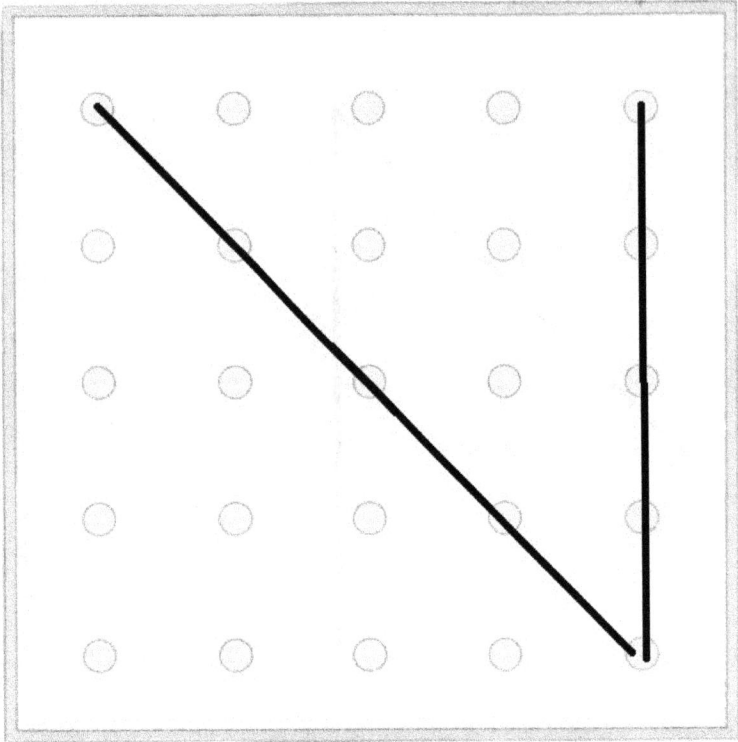

16

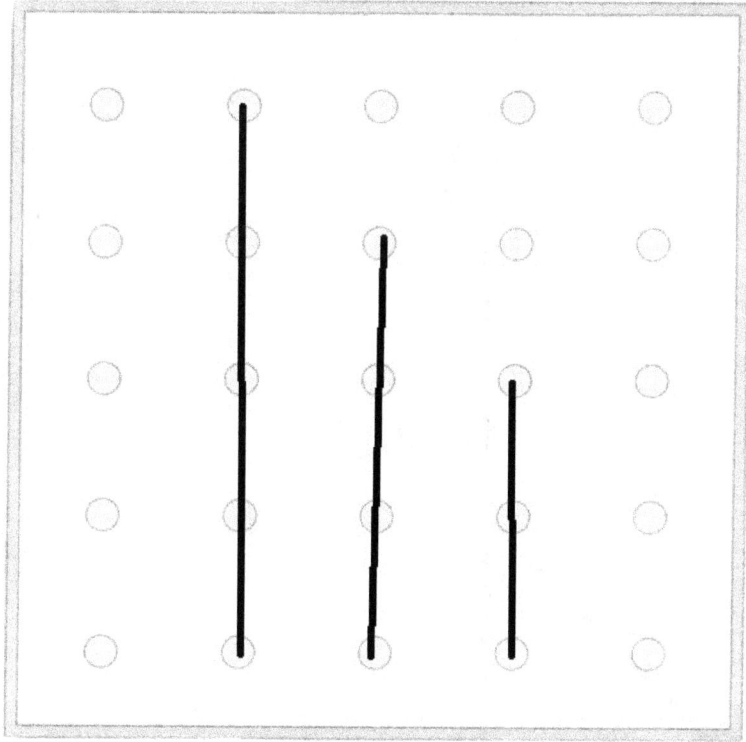

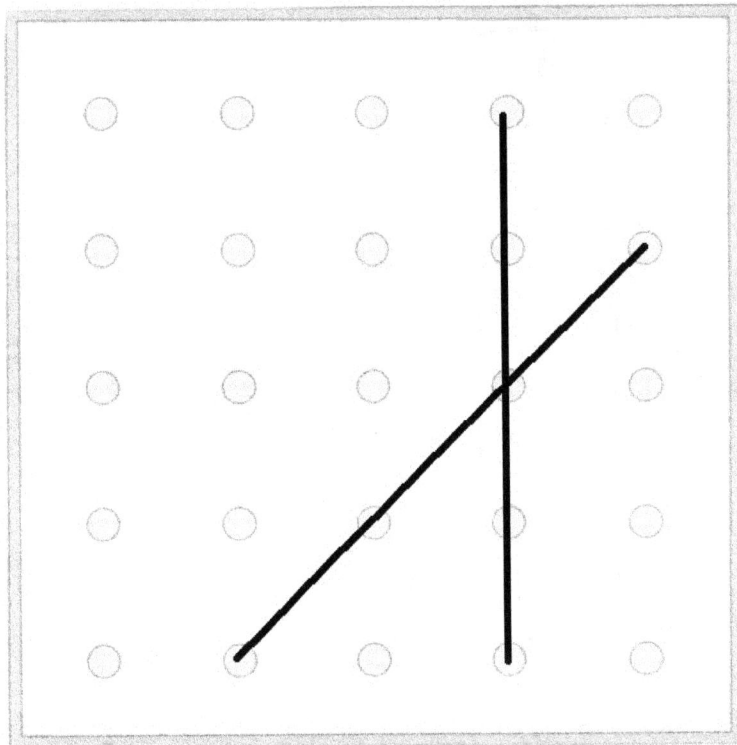

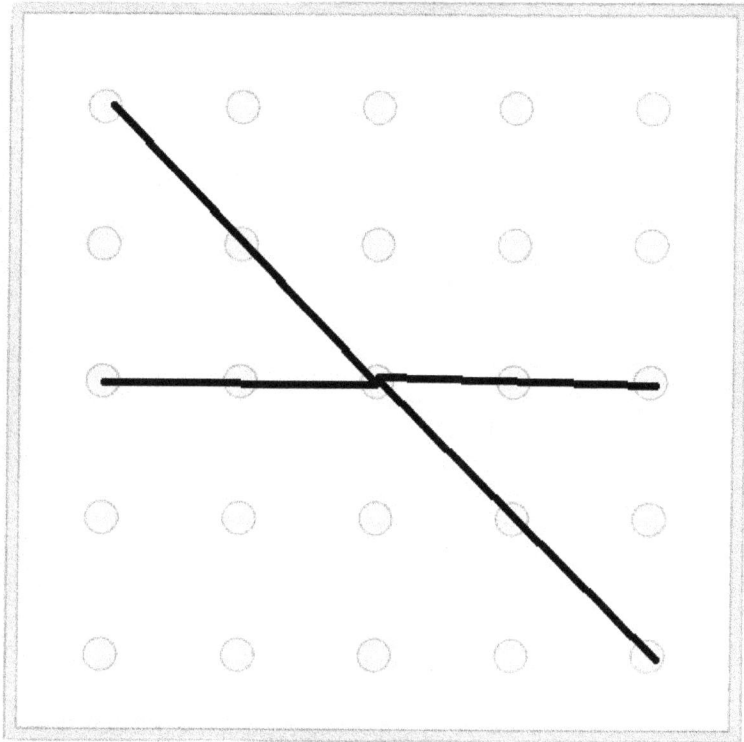

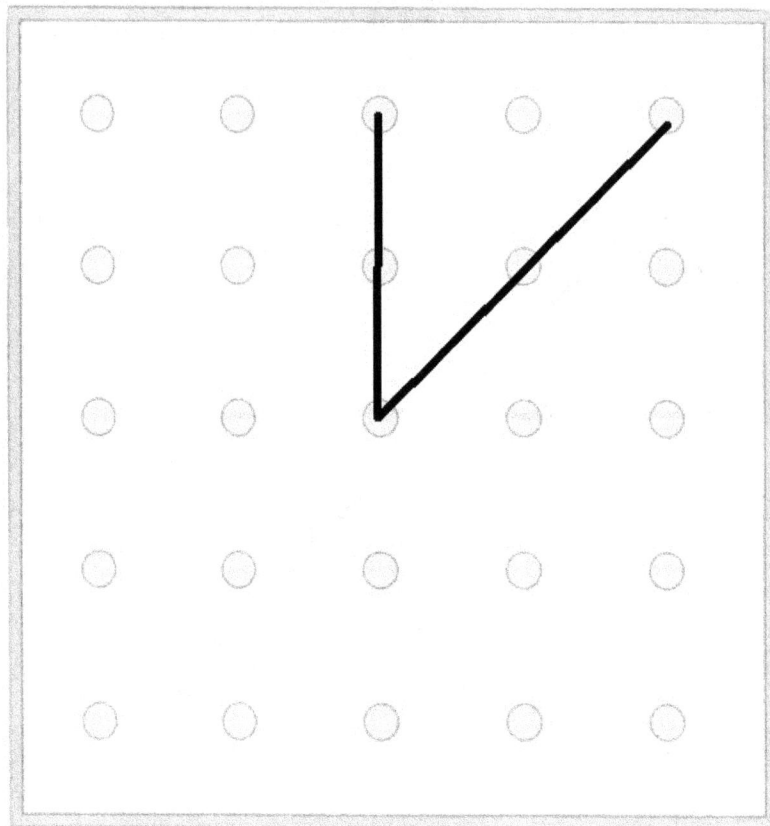

YEAH!!!!!

YOU finished this part of Level A and earned the privilege to advance to Level 1 !!

You are AWESOME!!!

LEVEL 1

YELLOW BOOK

Do you remember the directions from the level before this one? Before completing this design, I want you to answer some questions. First, how many rubber bands will you need to complete this challenge? ...OK. Next, where are you going to start? ...What will be your next step? Tell me the moves all the way to the finish. Do you think you will be able to complete this design?"

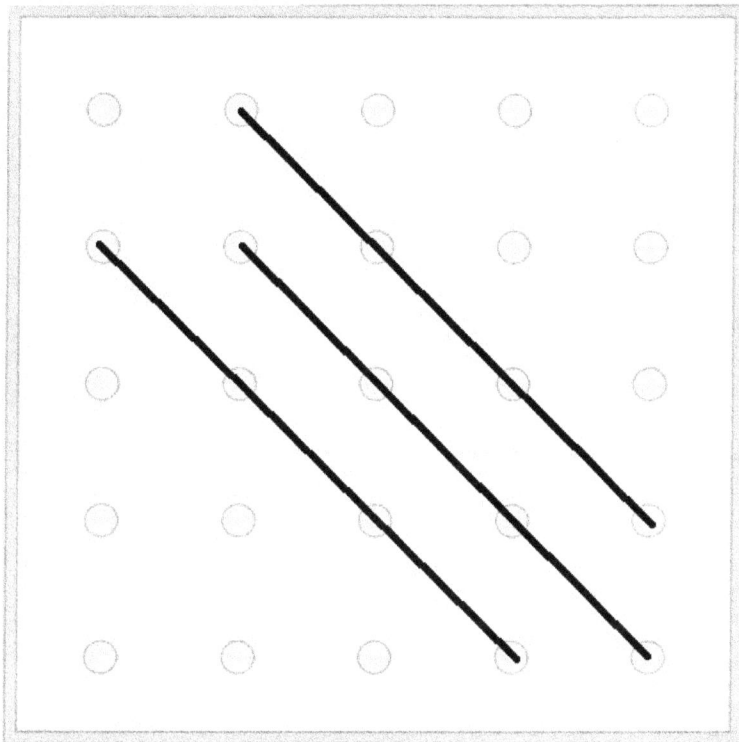

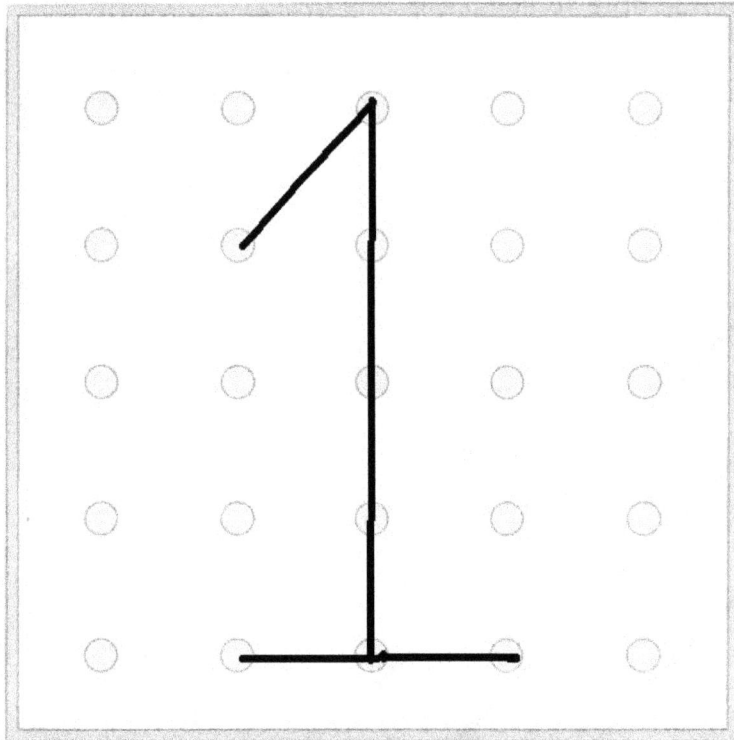

What does this look like?

24

Do the same thing on each of these pages. First, tell me how many rubber bands you will need to complete this challenge? Next, where are you going to start and the steps you will take to finish. Then let me know if you think you will be able to complete the design. If you are not sure, the best way to complete these challenges is to always count the pegs (or dots) on this page, count the pegs on the board, then use the rubber bands to make the design.

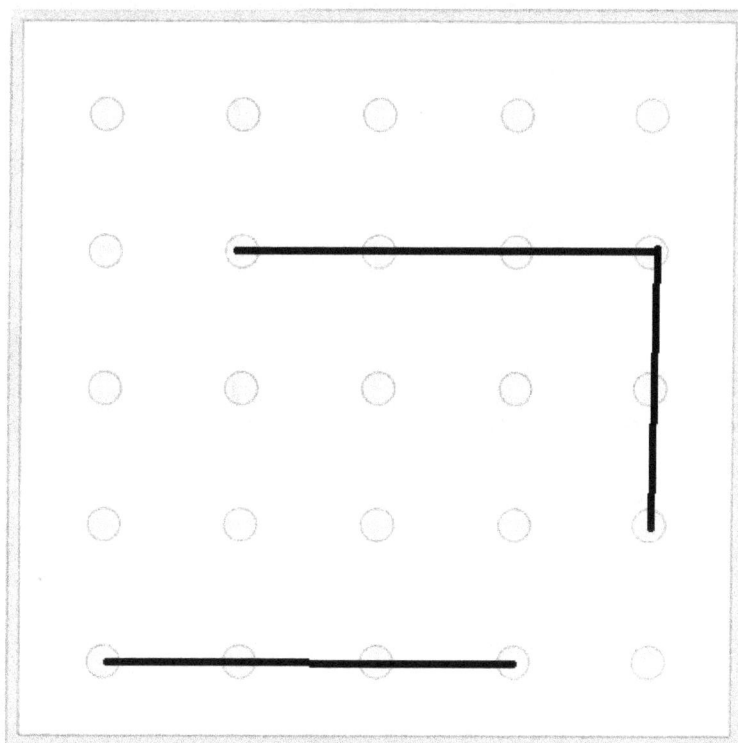

Do the same thing here. Talk to me about your plan to put the rubber bands in the correct positions. If you are not sure, count the pegs (or dots) on this page before starting to make your design.

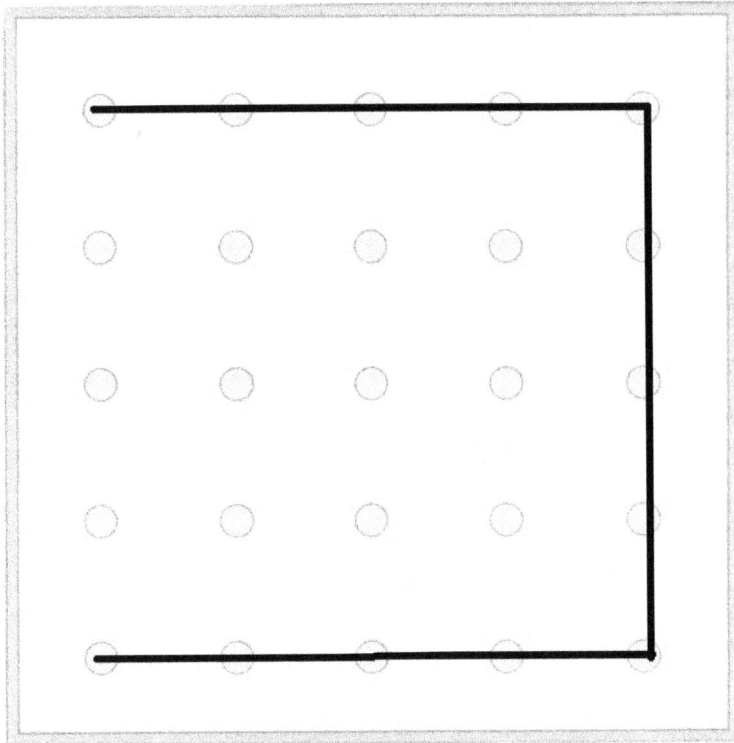

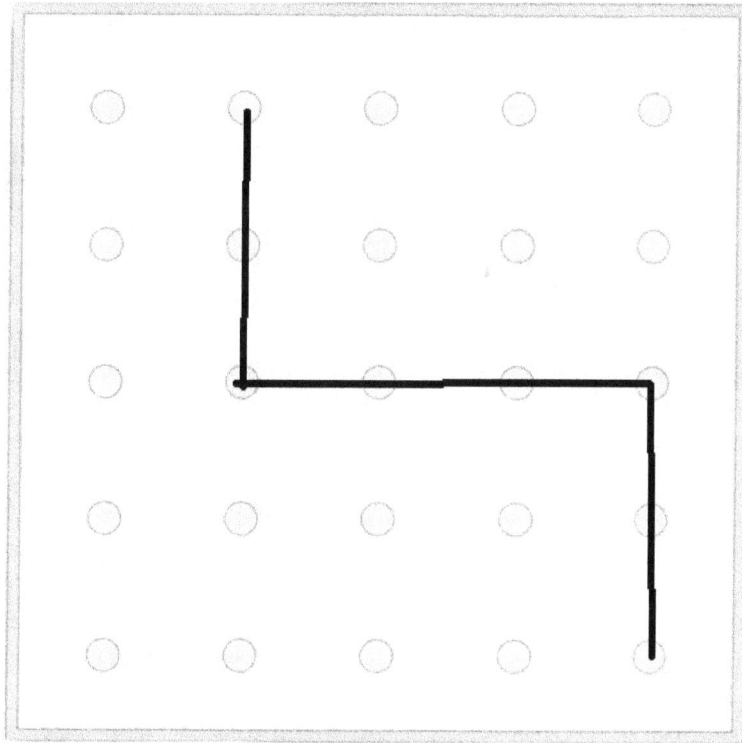

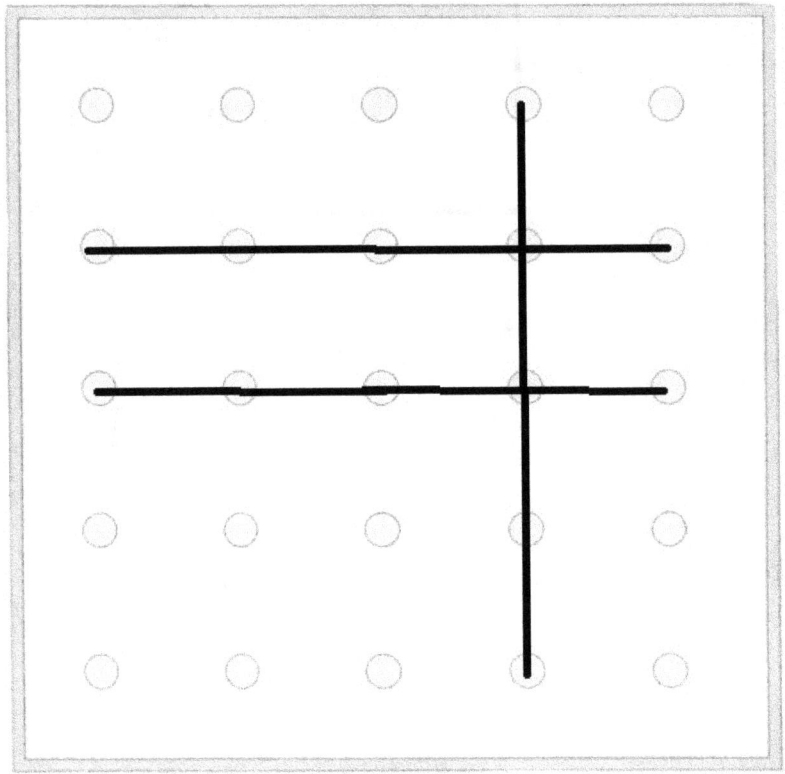

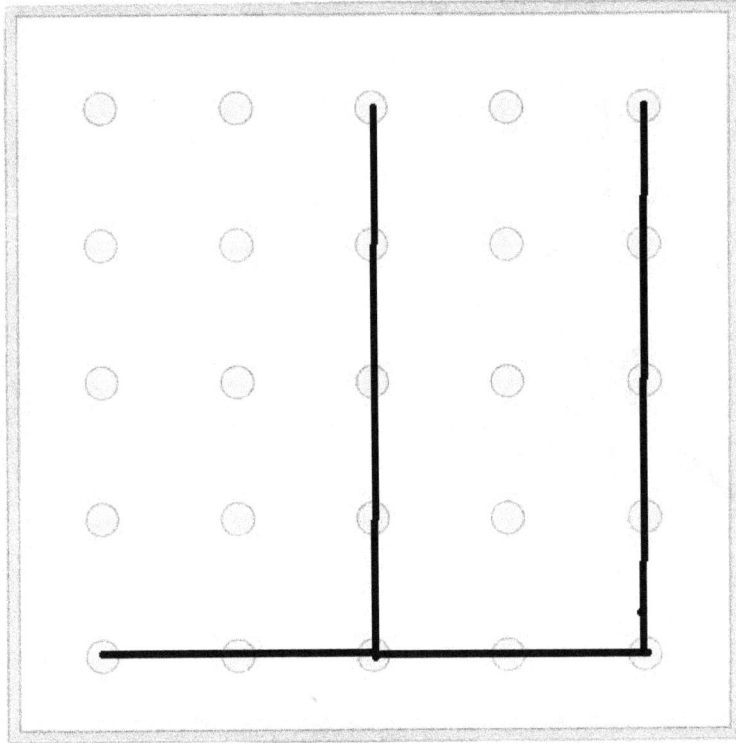

COUNT THE PEGS (DOTS) BEFORE MAKING YOUR DESIGN AND YOU WILL
ALWAYS BE CORRECT!

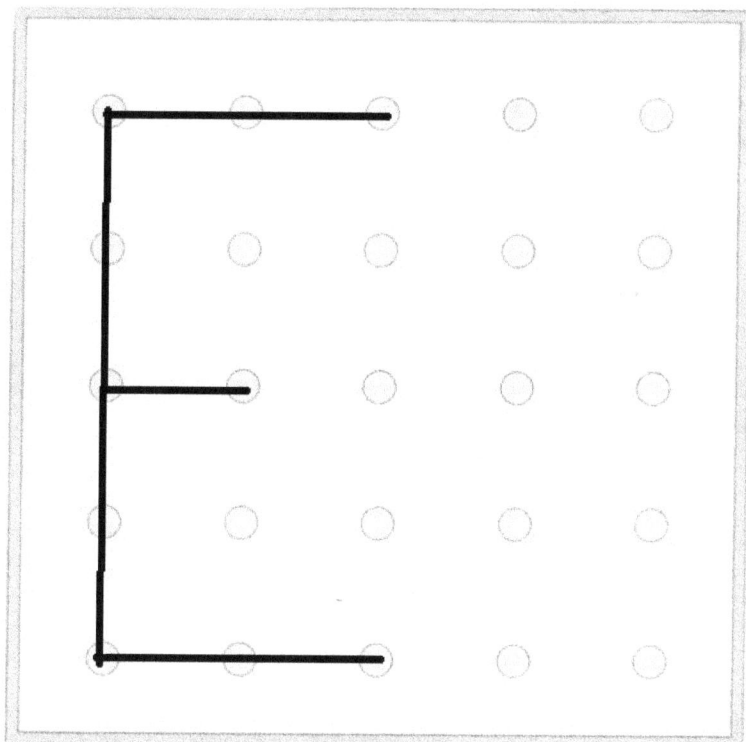

IS THERE AN "E" IN YOUR NAME?

WHAT LETTER DOES THIS LOOK LIKE?

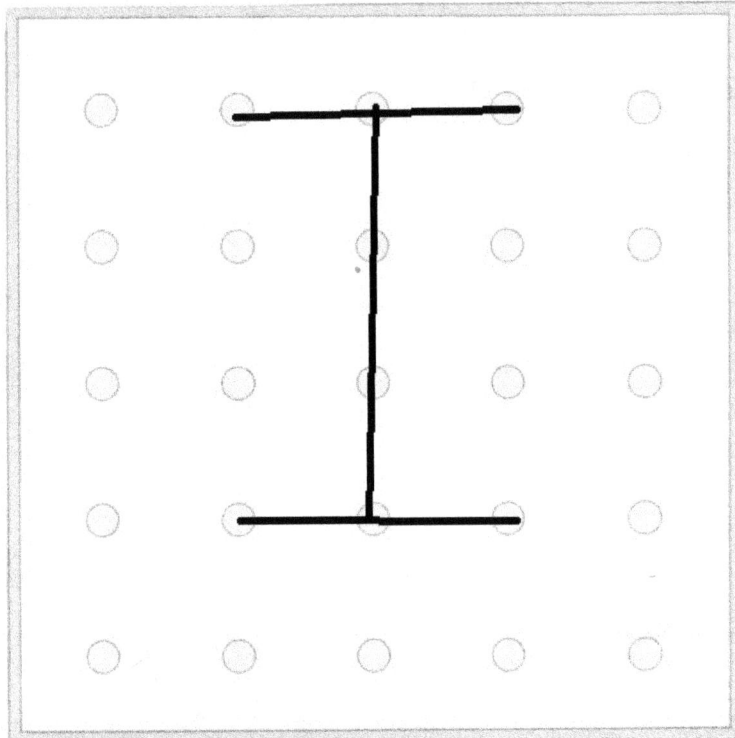

IS THERE AN "I" IN YOUR NAME?

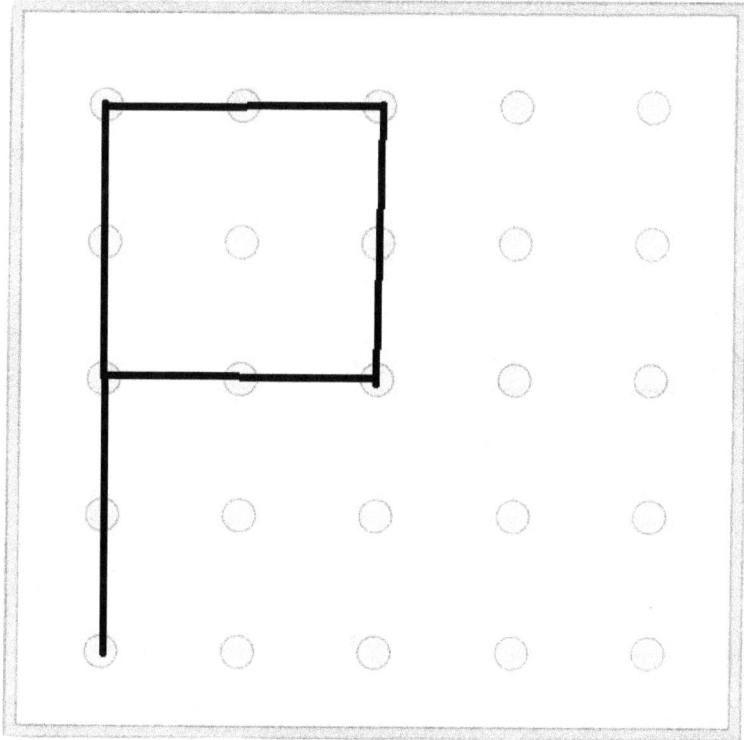

DOES THIS LOOK LIKE A LETTER?.....IS THERE AN "A" IN YOUR NAME?

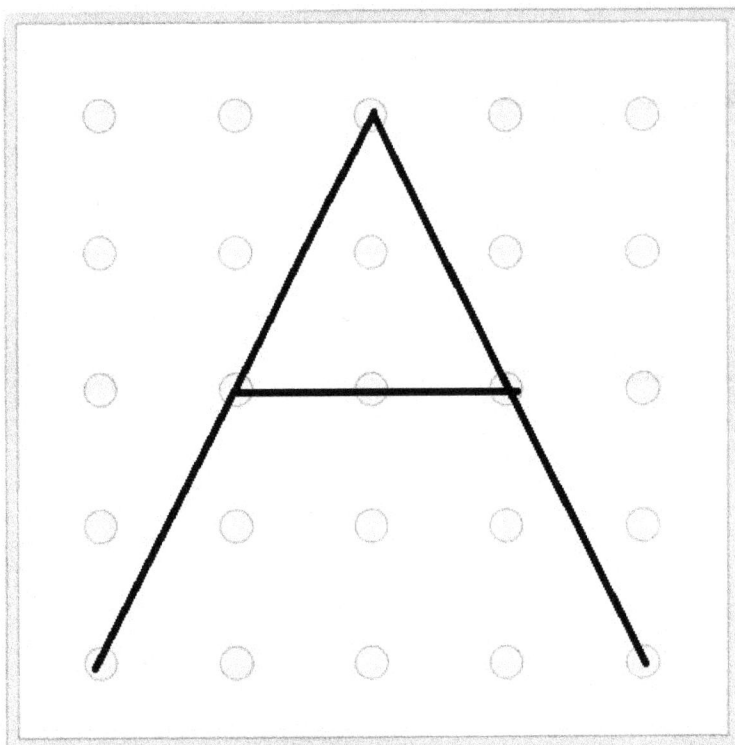

HOW ABOUT THIS? IS THIS A LETTER?

IS THERE AN "F" IN YOUR NAME?

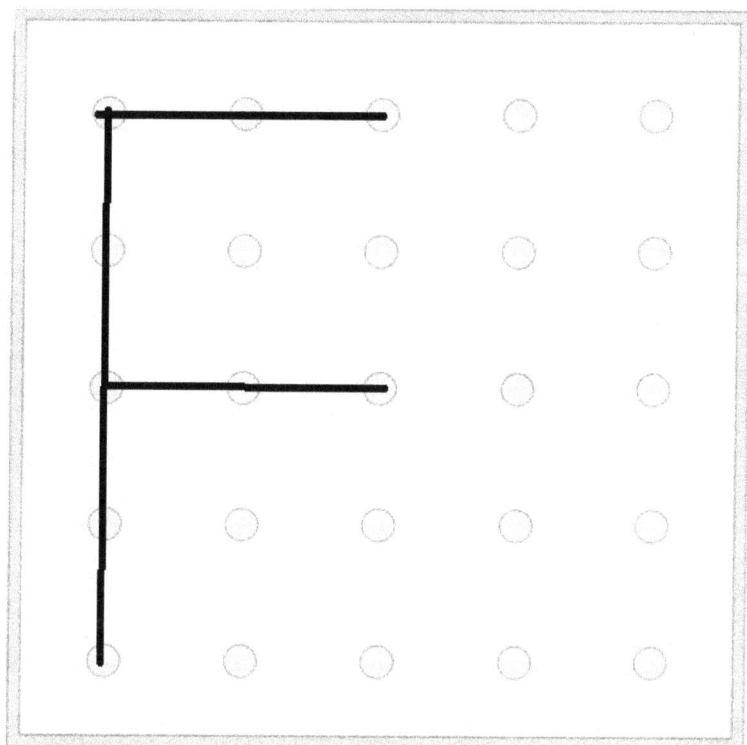

WHAT LETTER DOES THIS LOOK LIKE?.....CAN YOU TELL ME A WORD THAT
BEGINS WITH "N"?

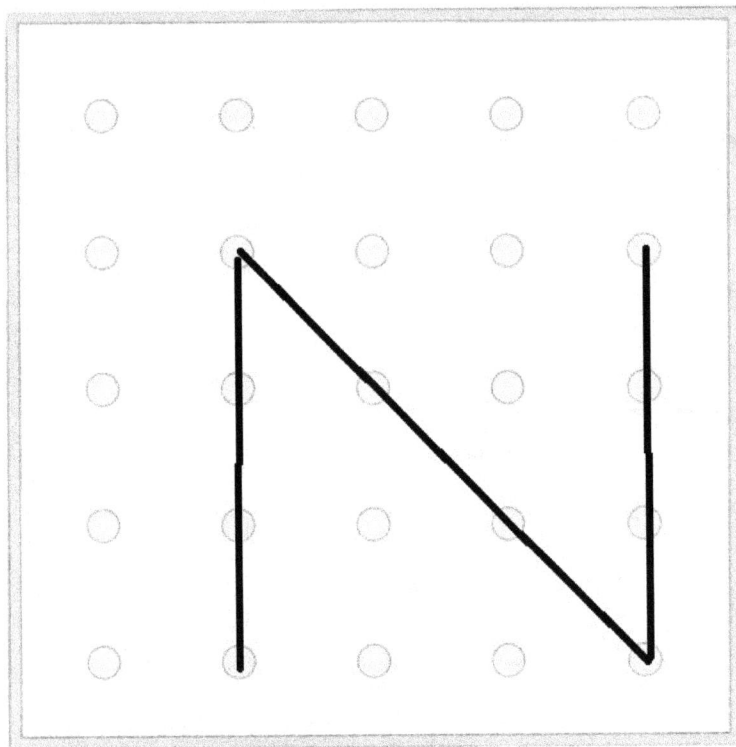

REMEMBER TELL ME YOUR PLAN AND COUNT THE PEGS BEFORE YOU START
MAKING A PLAN IF THAT HELPS.

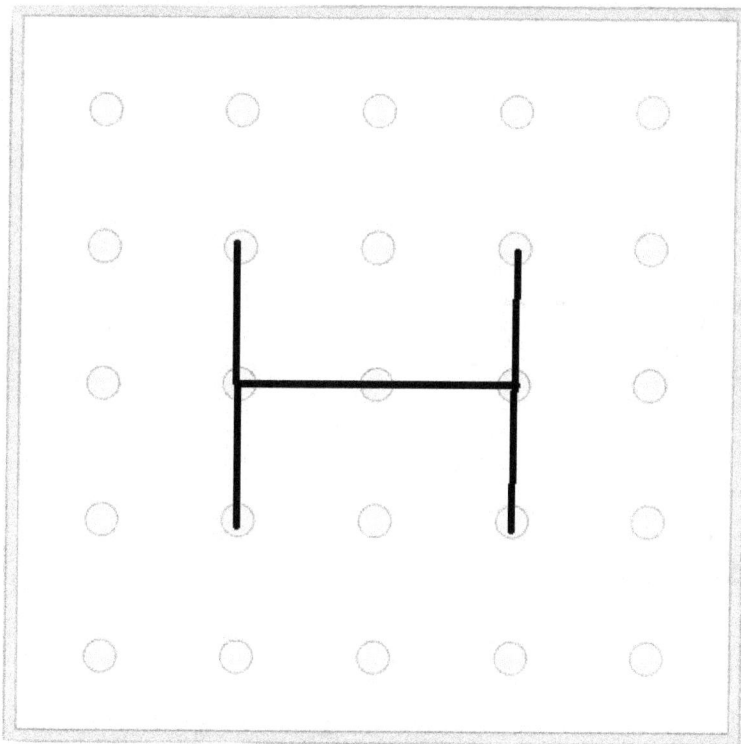

WHAT LETTER DOES THIS LOOK LIKE?...IS THERE AN "H" IN YOUR NAME?

HOW ABOUT THIS? WHAT LETTER IS THIS? IS THERE A "Z" IN YOUR NAME? CAN YOU THINK OF A WORD THAT BEGINS WITH "Z"?

HOW ABOUT THIS? WHAT LETTER IS THIS? IS THERE A "U" IN YOUR NAME? CAN YOU THINK OF A WORD THAT BEGINS WITH "U"?

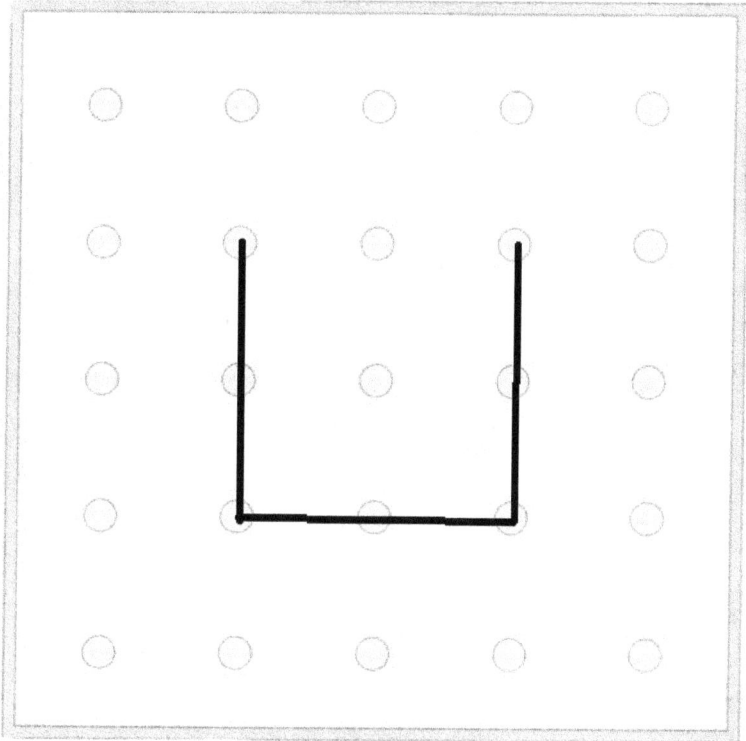

WHAT IS THIS SHAPE CALLED?

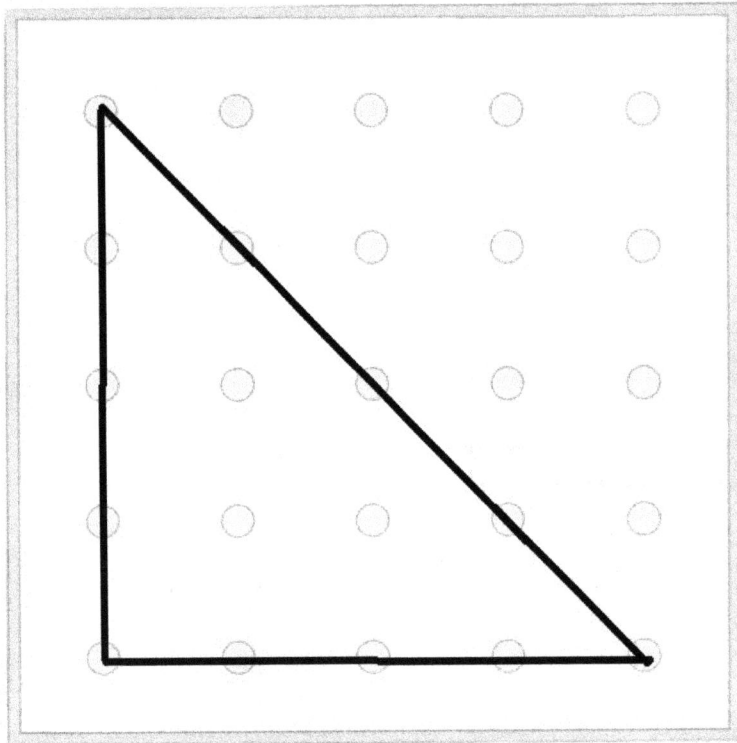

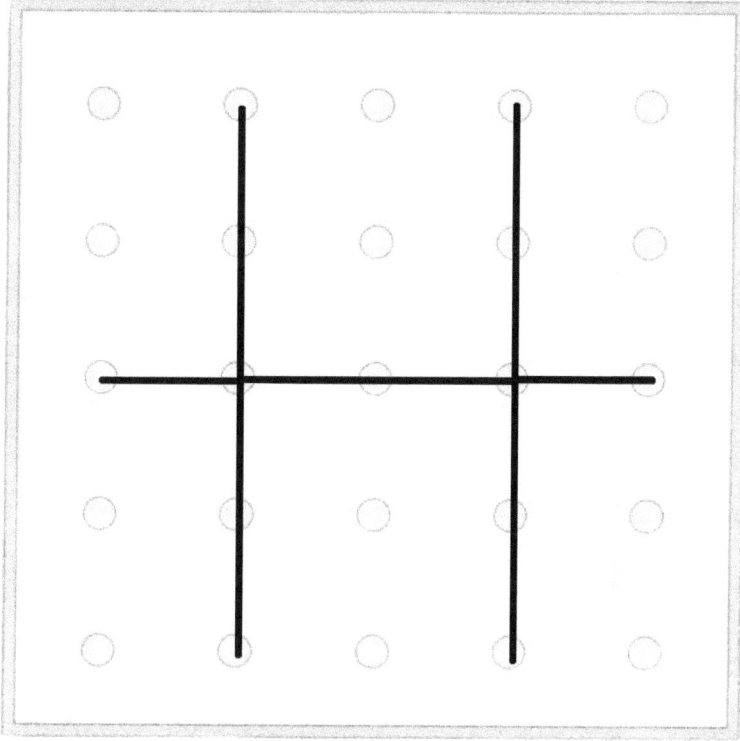

Always start with a plan!!

41

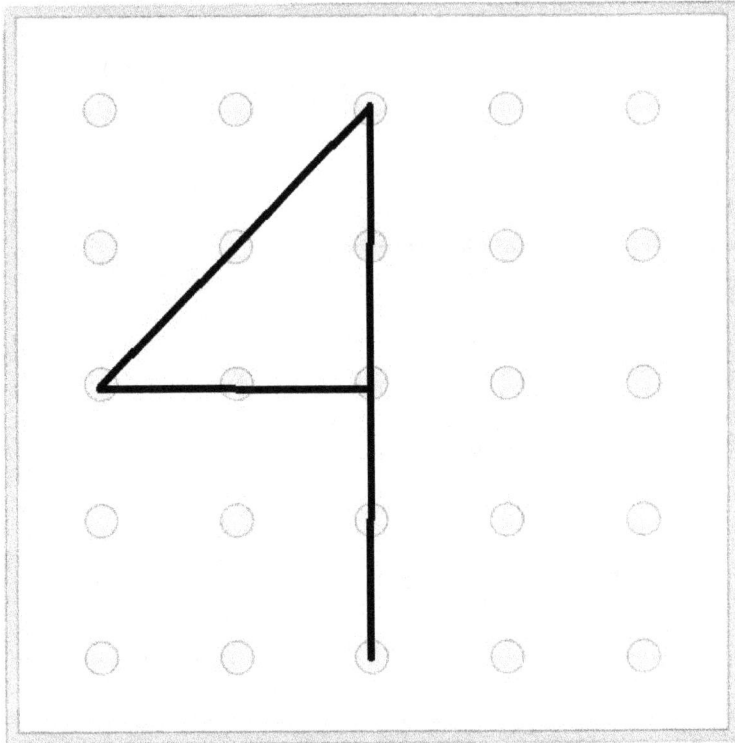

YEAH!!!!!

YOU finished this part of Level 1 and are now ready to return to the First Book and Begin Level 2.

LEVEL 2

"By now you have an idea of what you are supposed to do in order to be successful at these challenges. For the rest of these challenges, you will be asked to first complete the design. Then you will be asked to complete the design with the fewest rubber bands you POSSIBLY can. Many of these designs can be completed with only one rubber band....try it!!

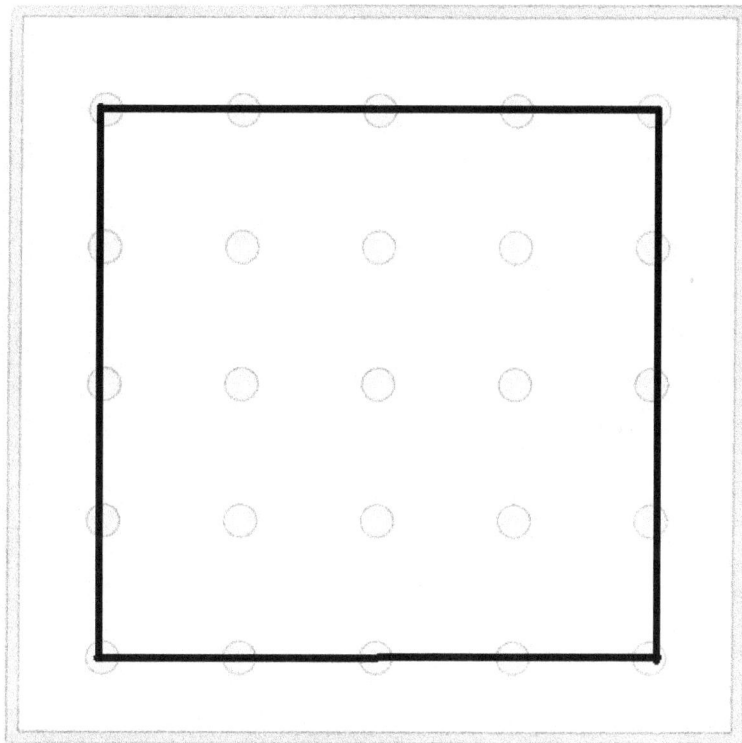

YOU WILL NEED MORE THAN ONE RUBBER BAND TO COMPLETE THIS
CHALLENGE!

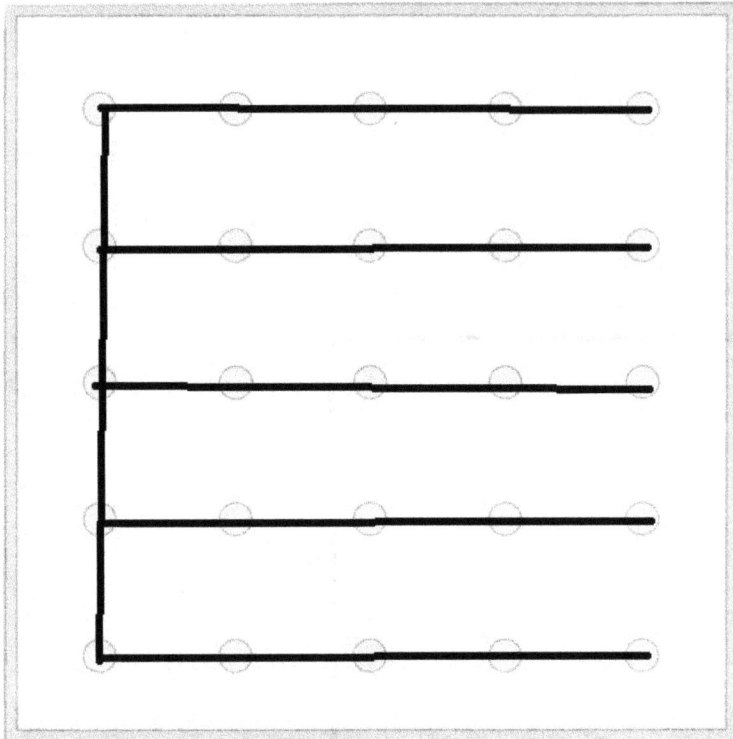

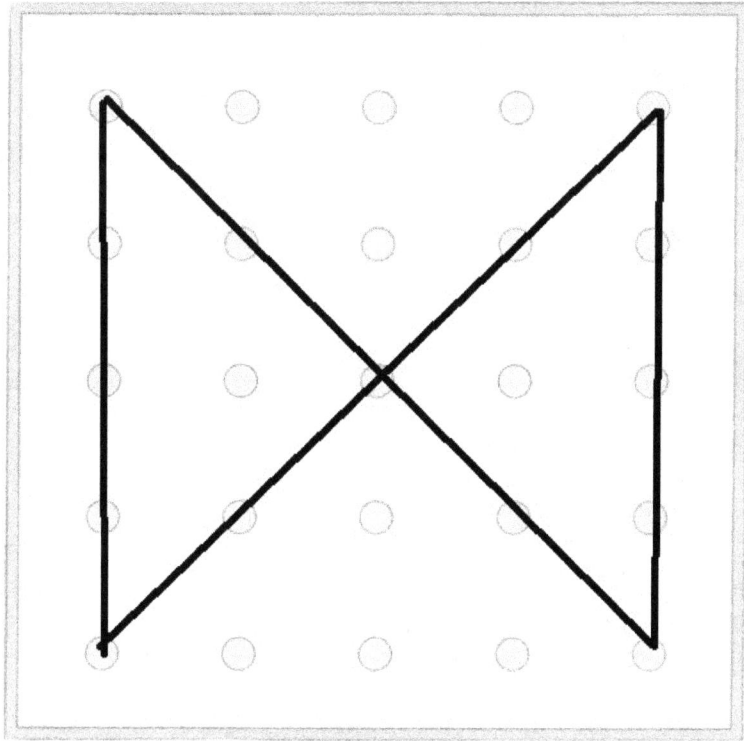

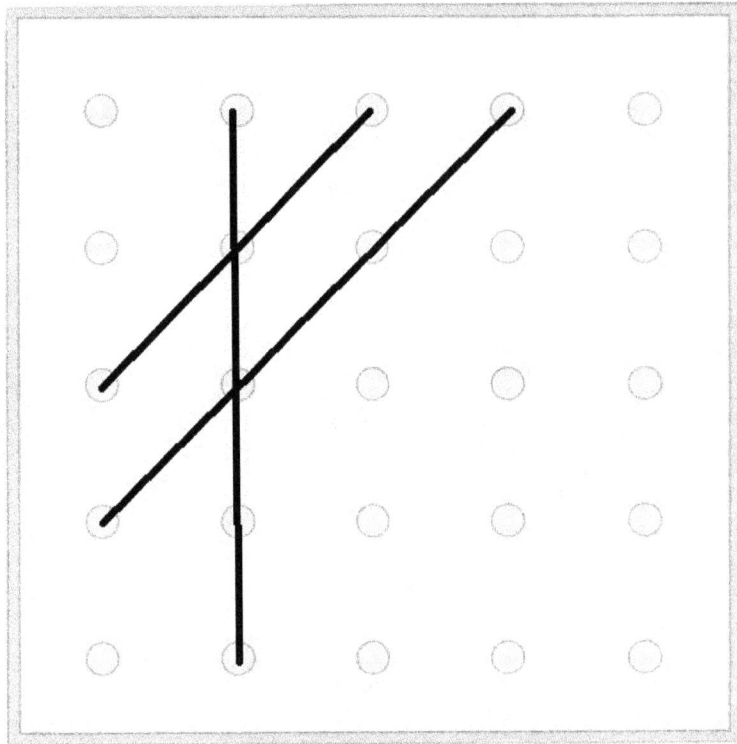

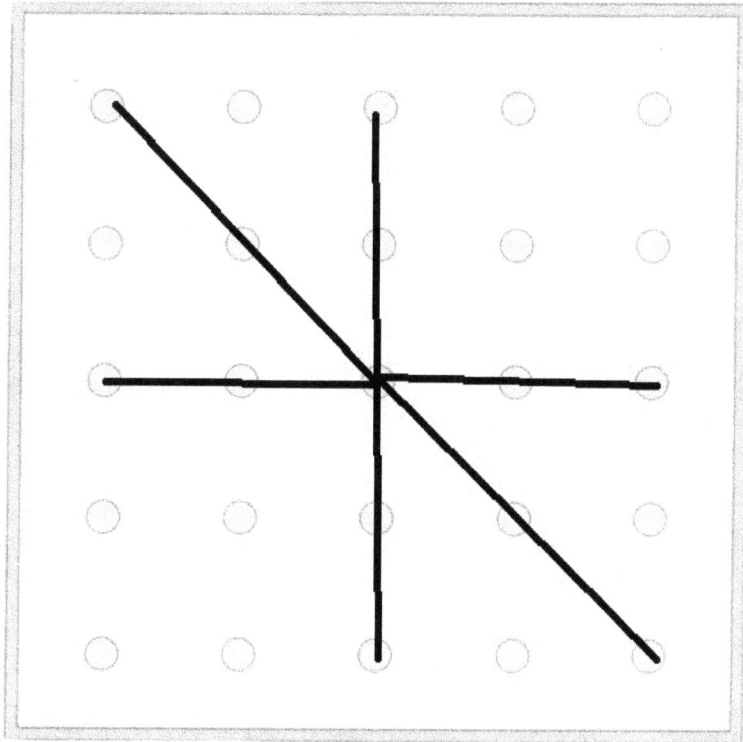

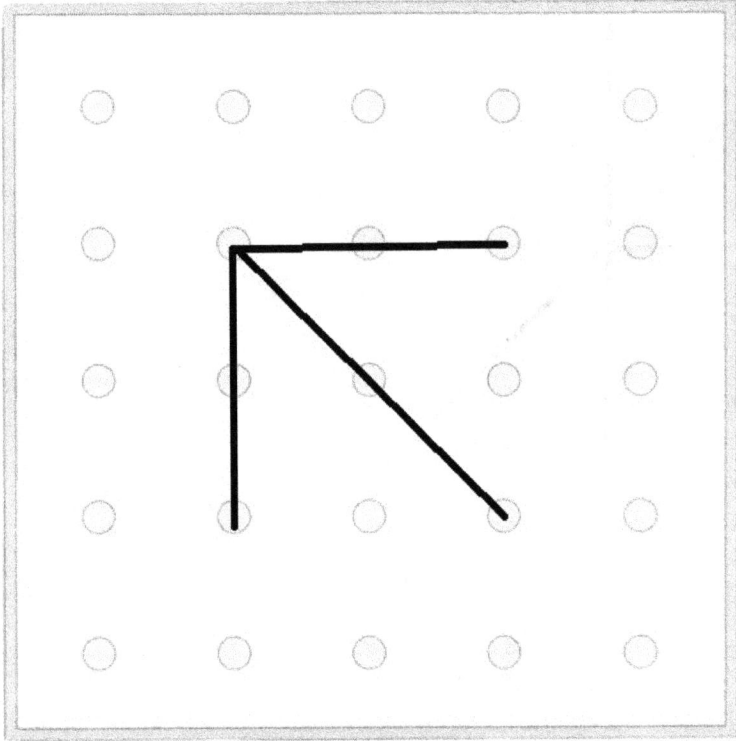

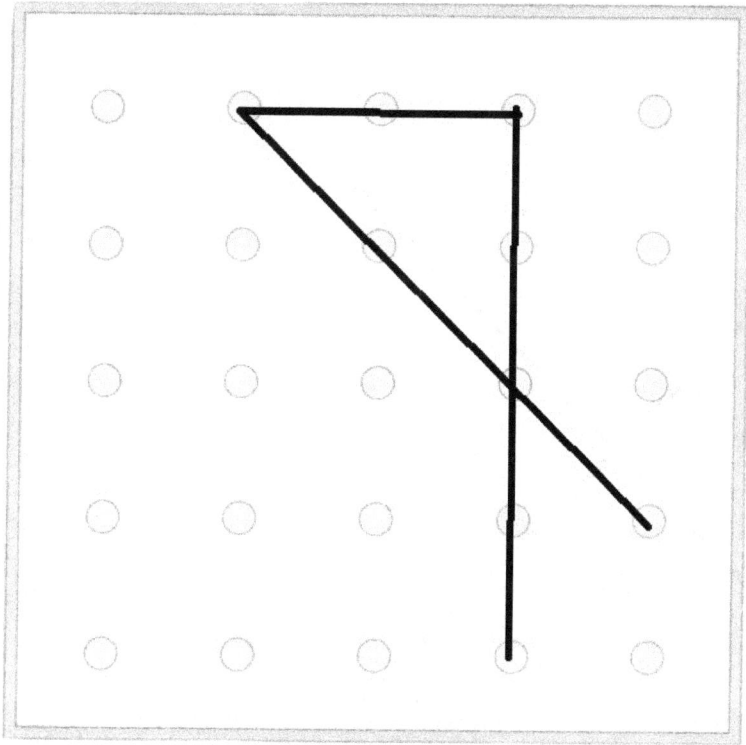

You are hopping right through these

53

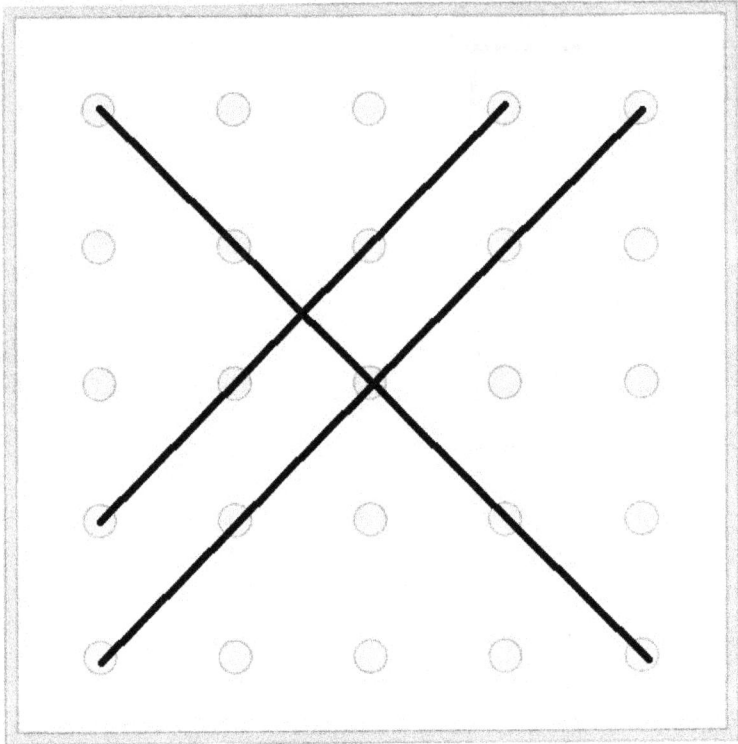

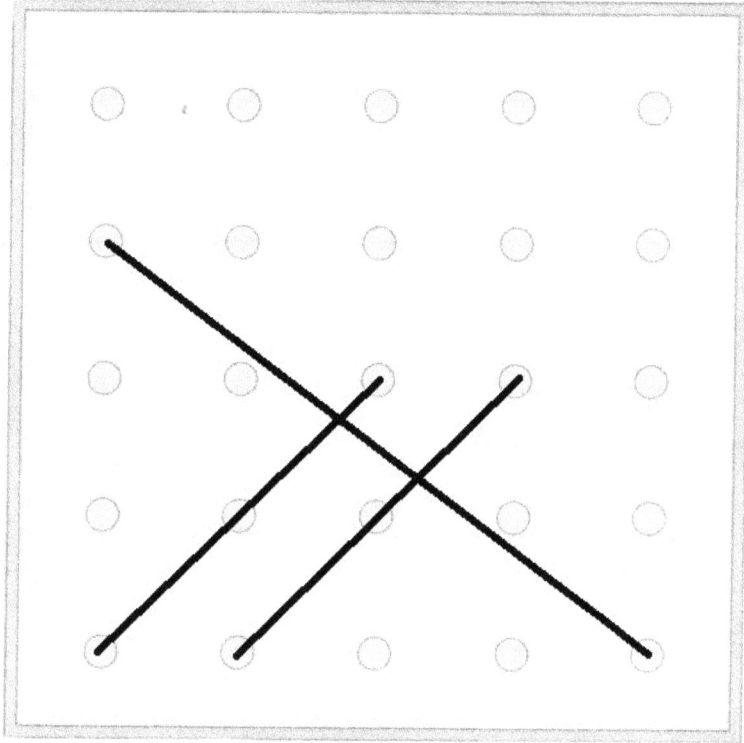

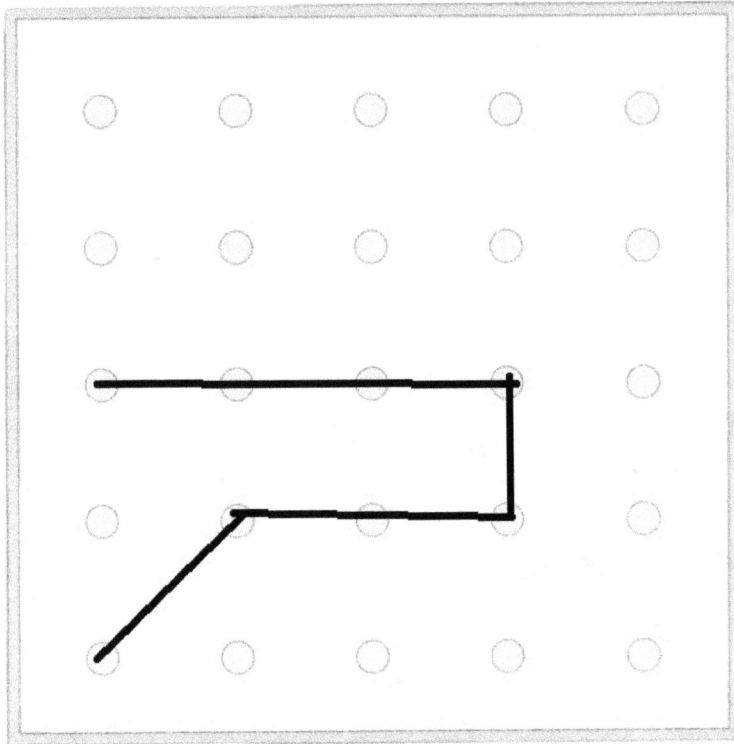

SHOW ME HOW TO MAKE THIS DESIGN WITH ONLY ONE RUBBER BAND.

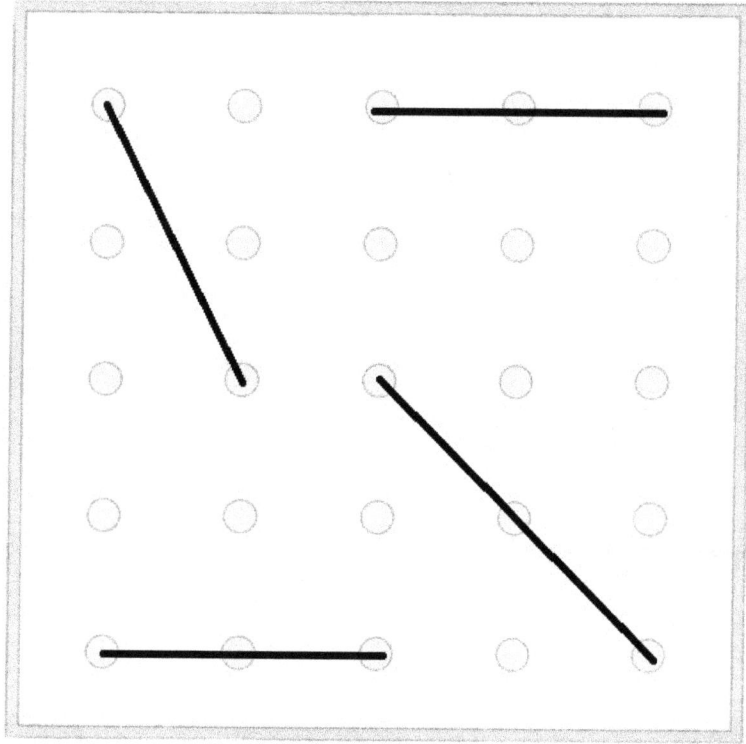

THIS IS ANOTHER DESIGN THAT ONLY NEEDS ONE RUBBER BAND TO COMPLETE.

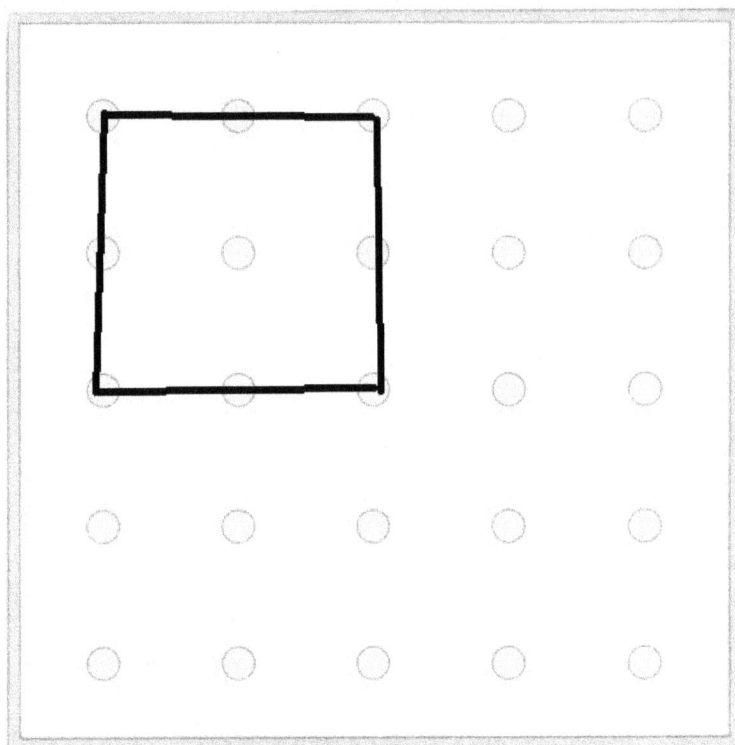

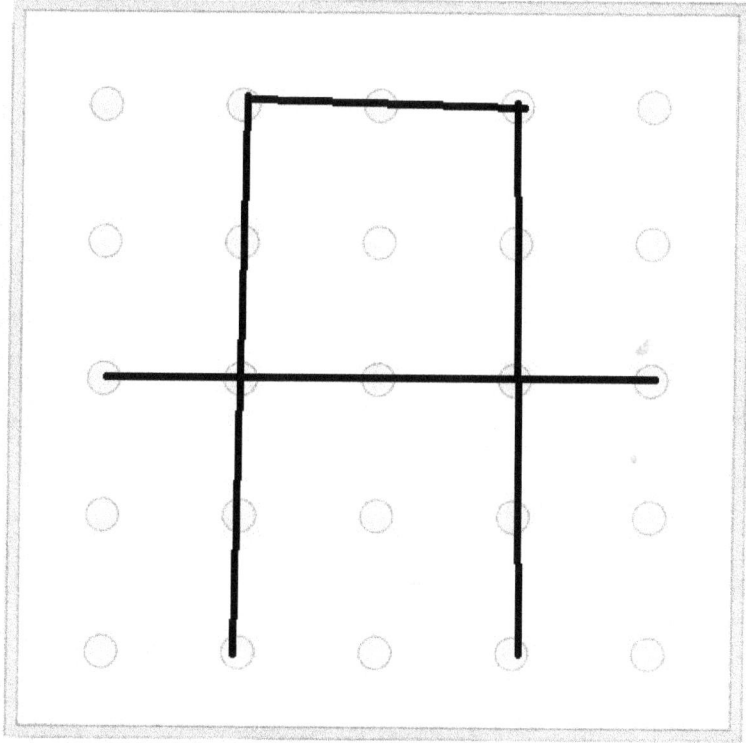

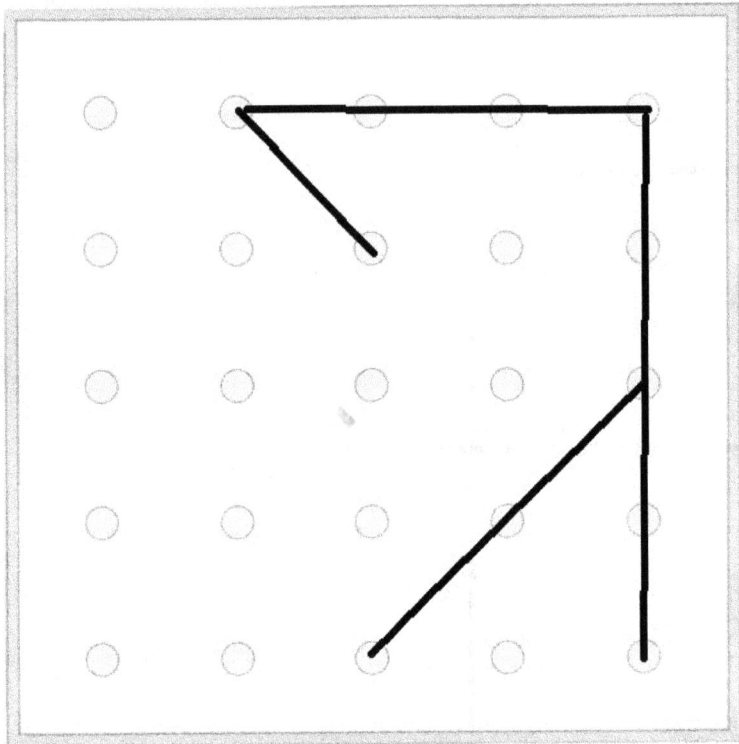

60

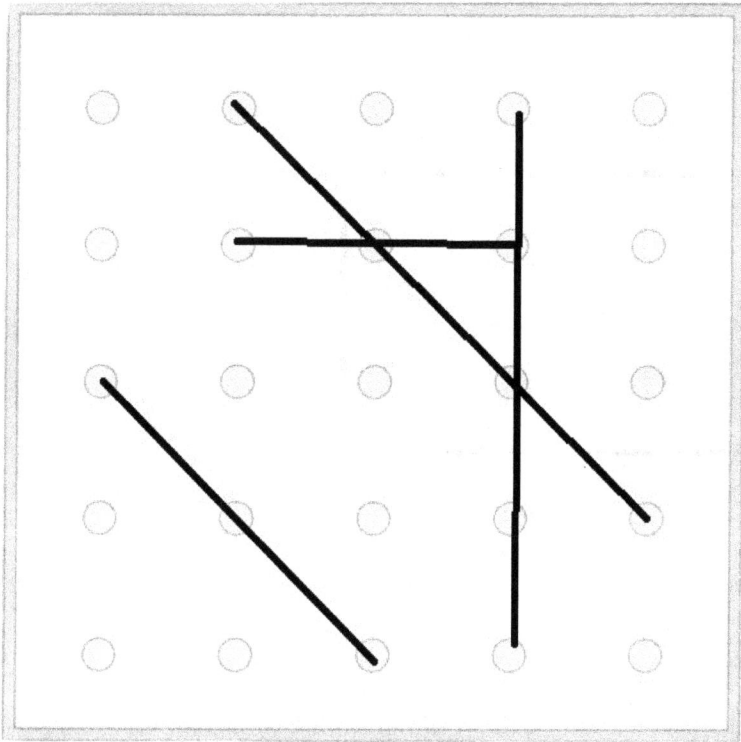

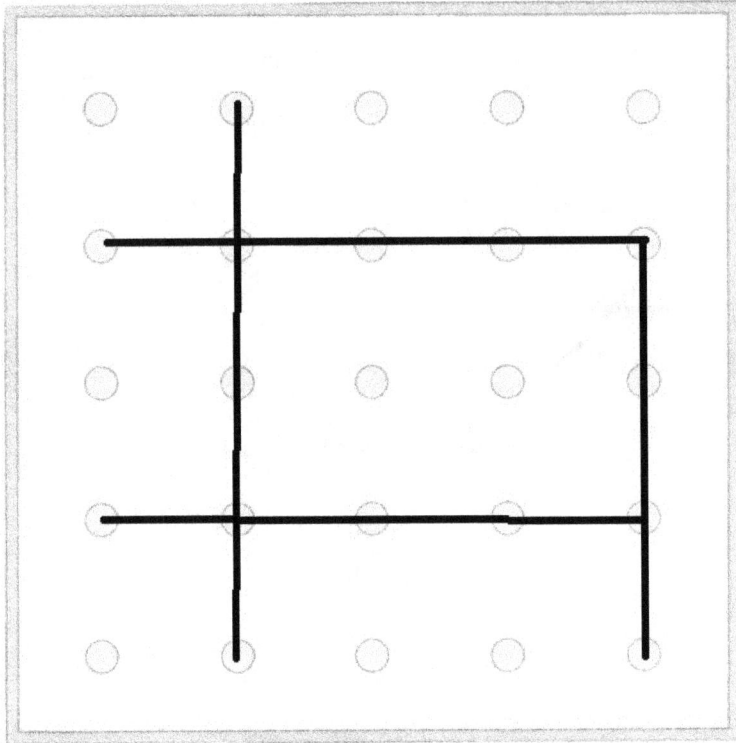

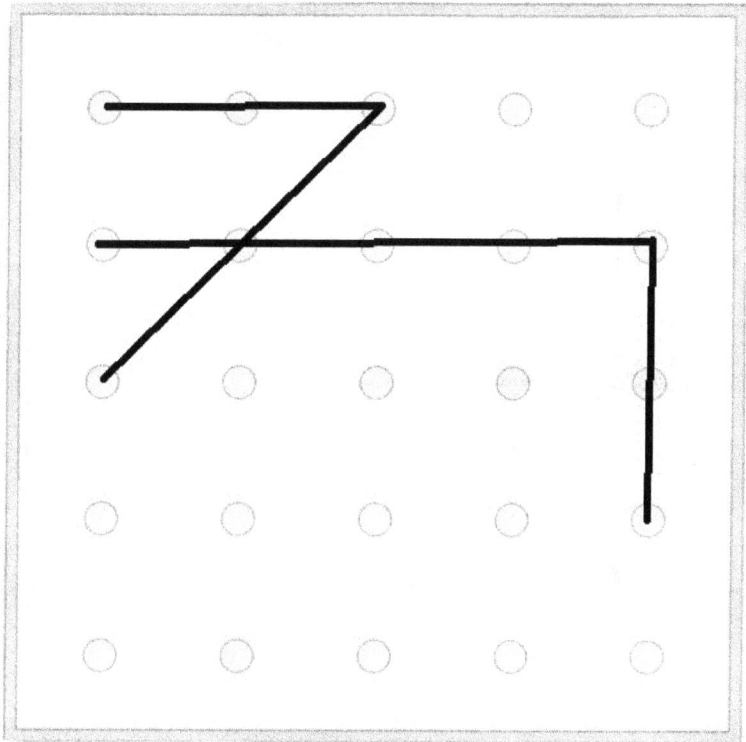

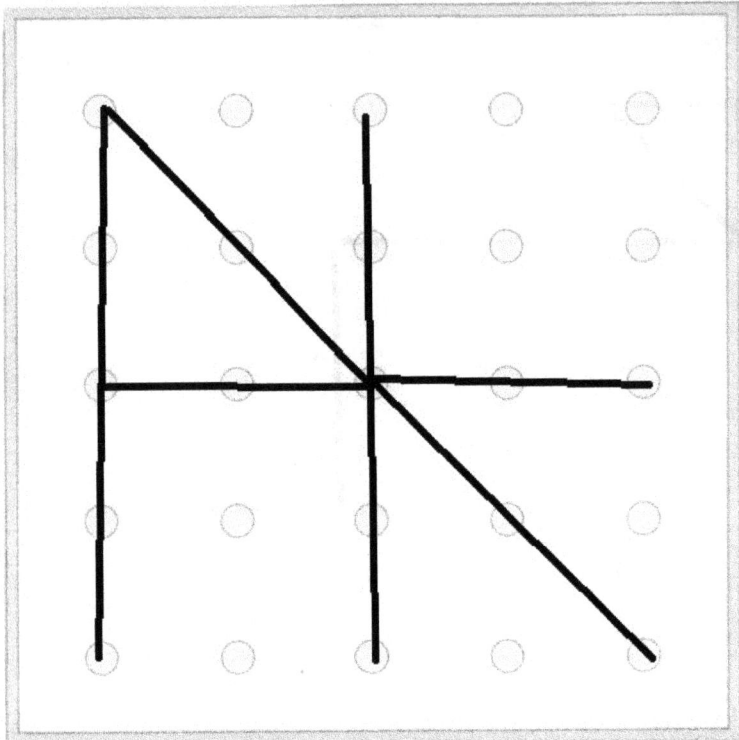

LEVEL 3

IN ORDER TO COMPLETE THIS CHALLENGE CORRECTLY, IT WILL BE VERY
IMPORTANT TO COUNT THE PEGS BEFORE YOU START!

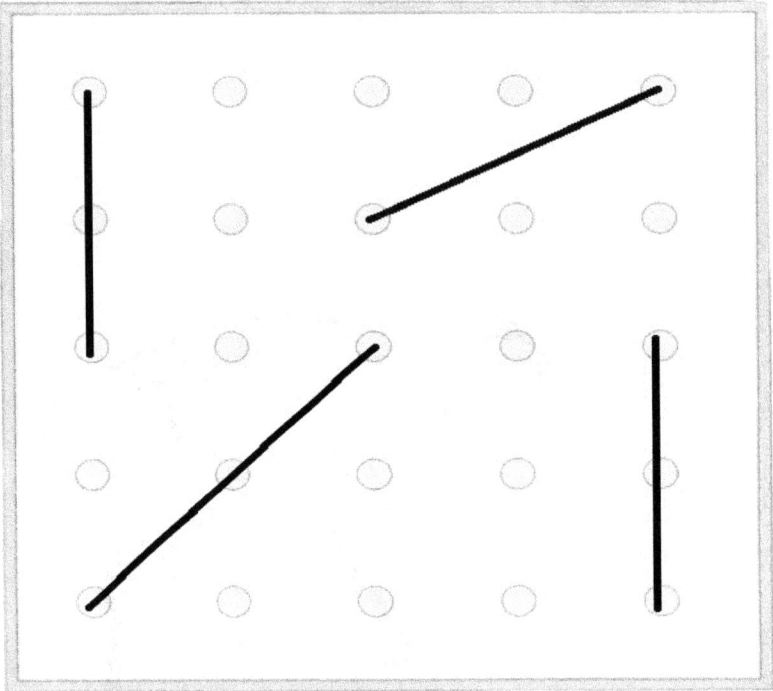

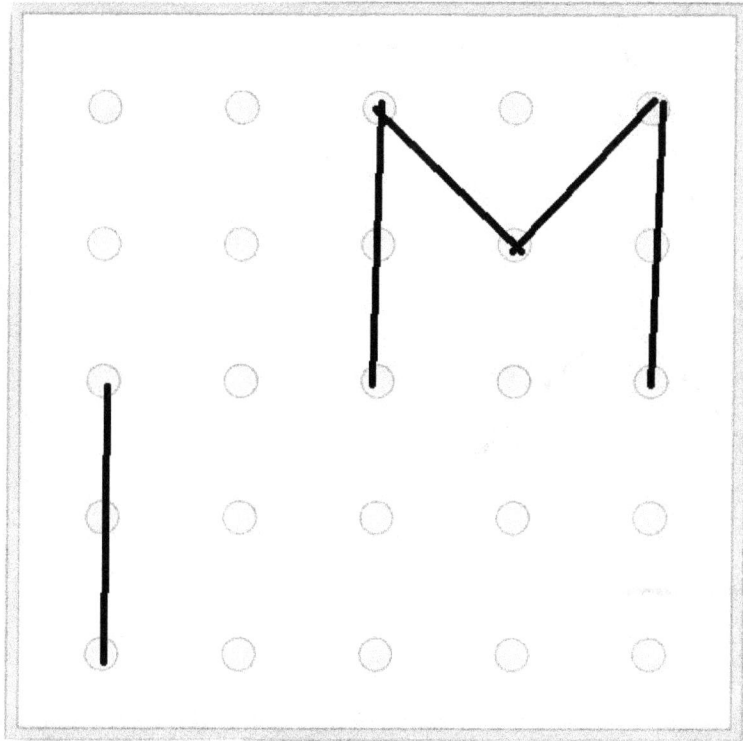

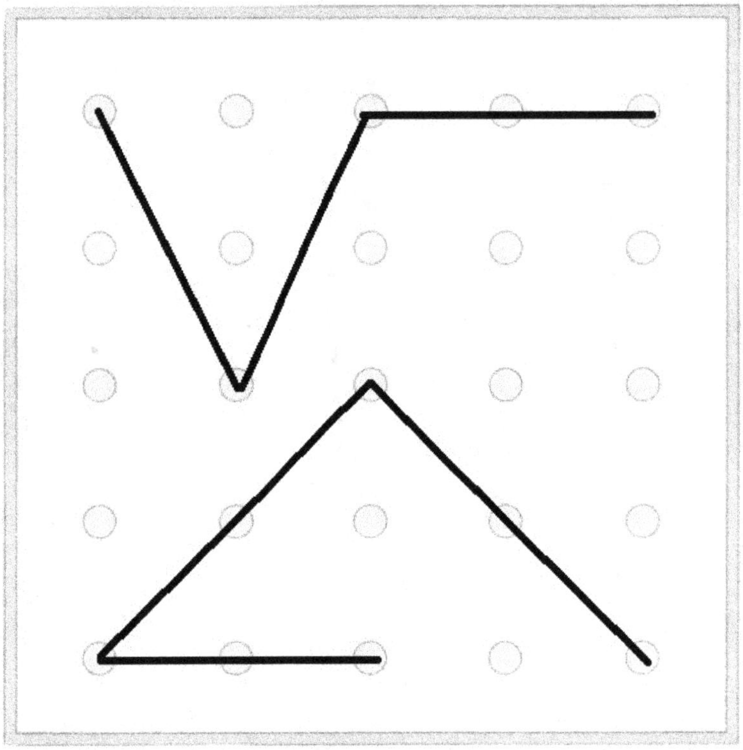

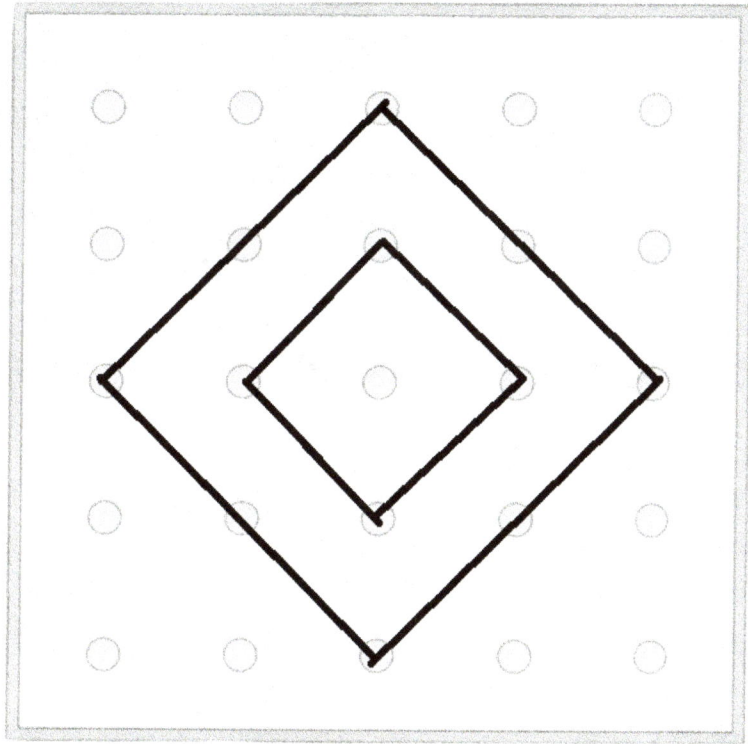

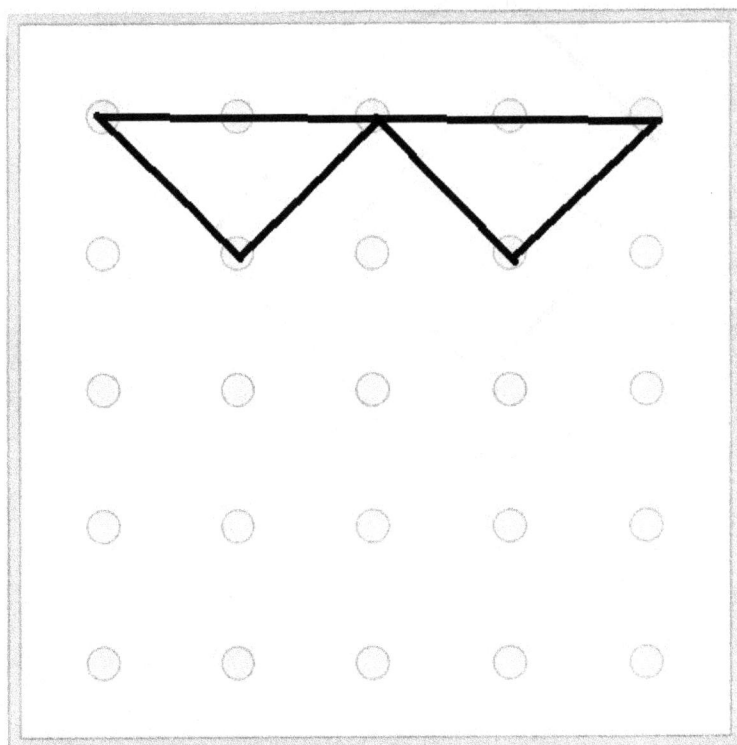

72

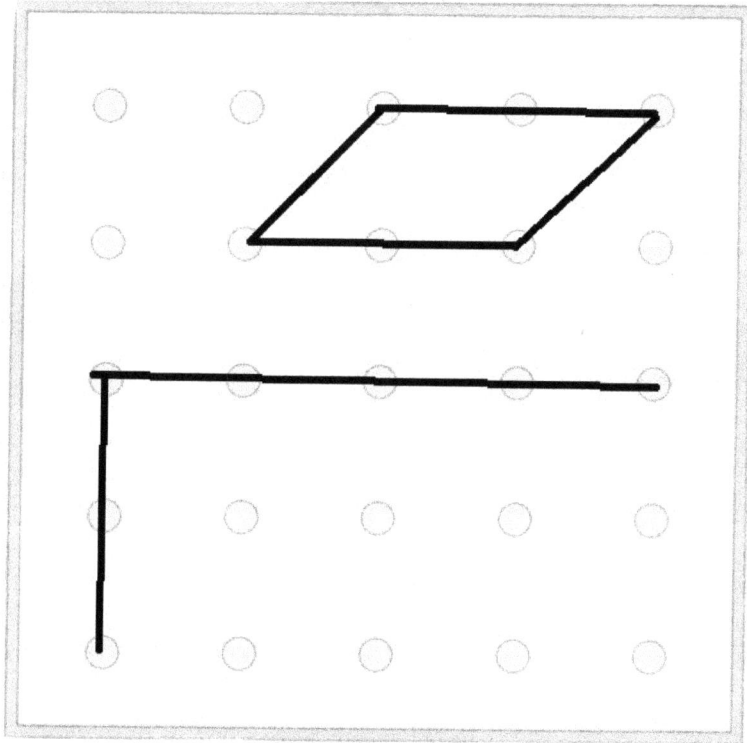

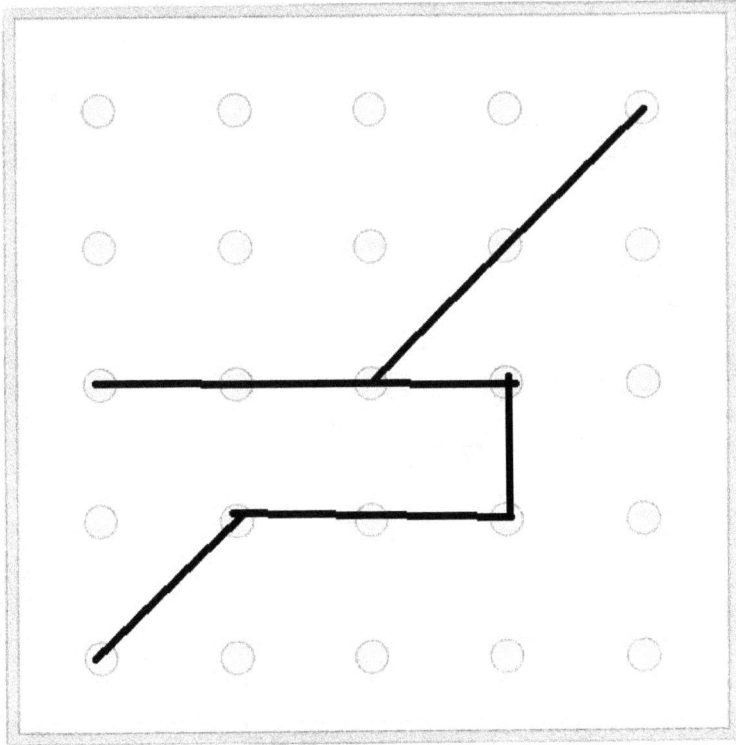

74

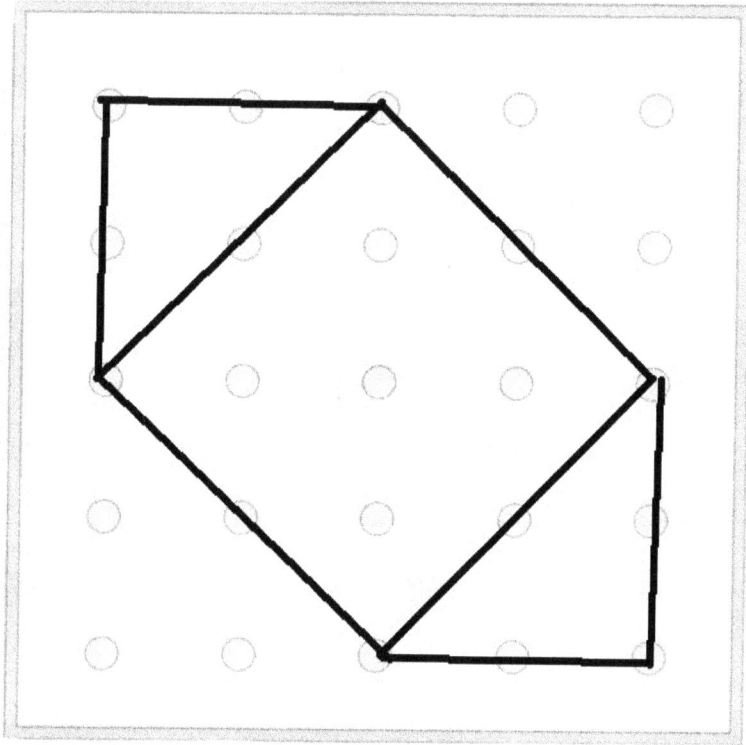

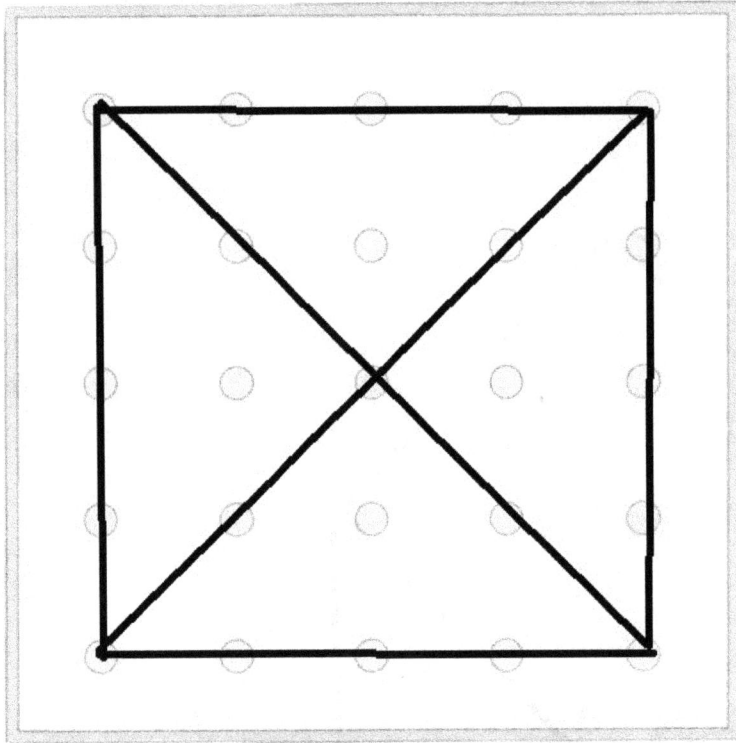

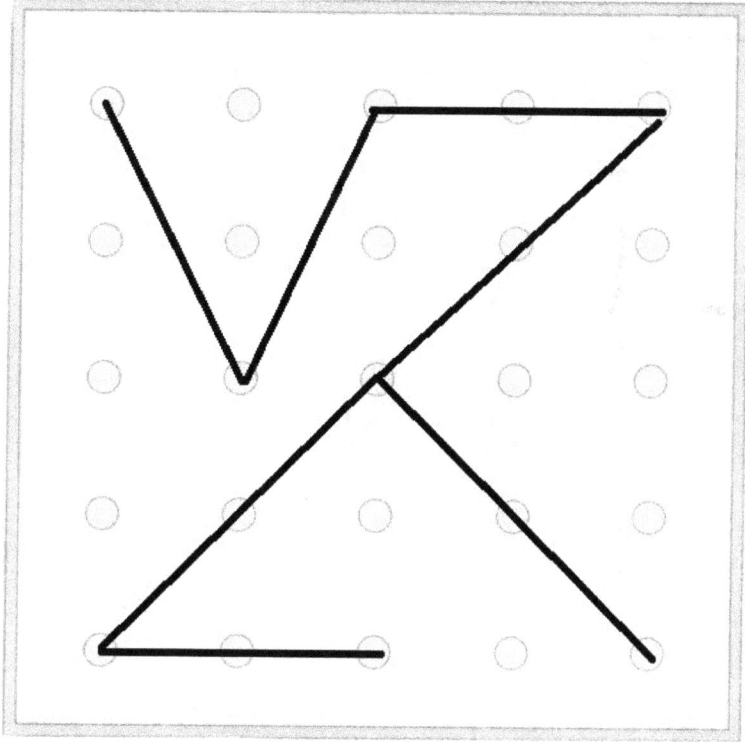

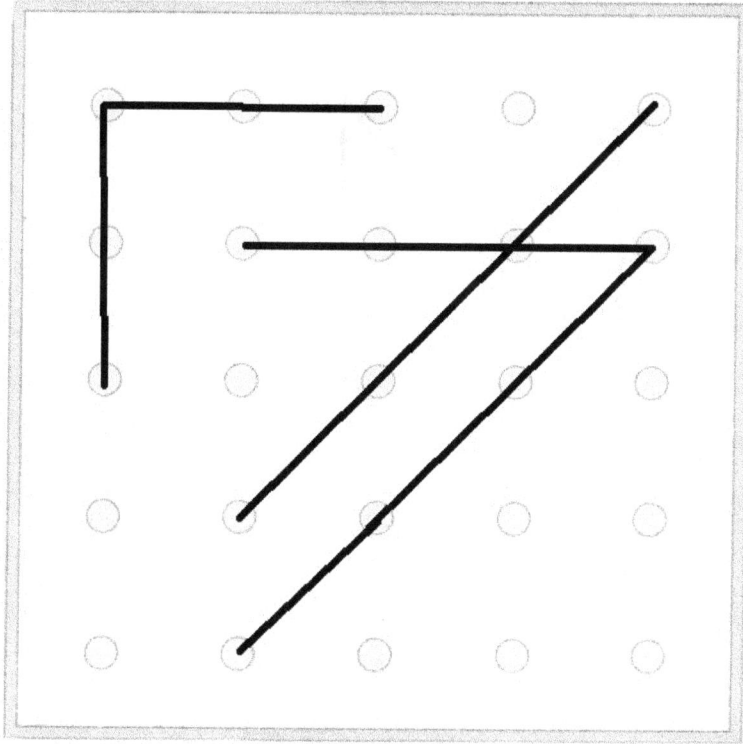

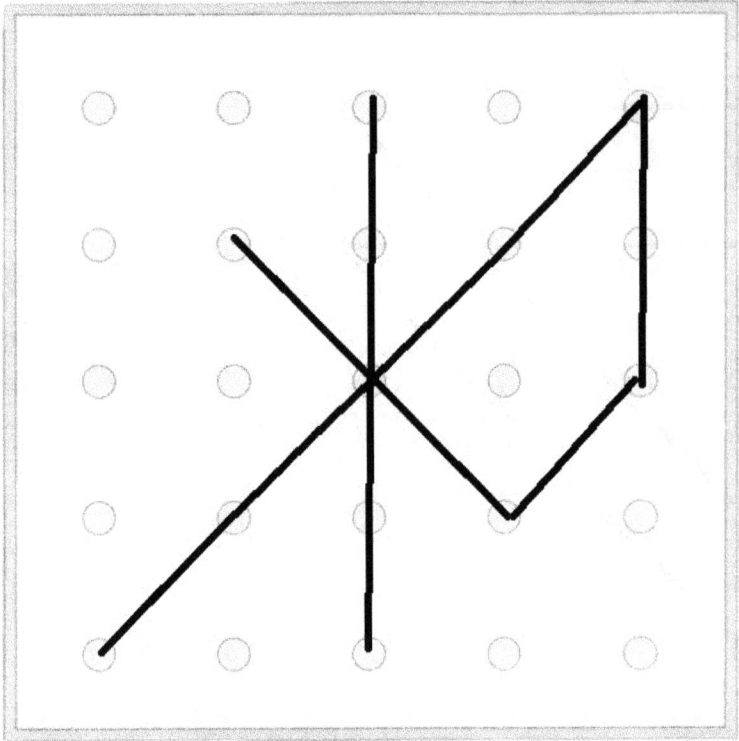

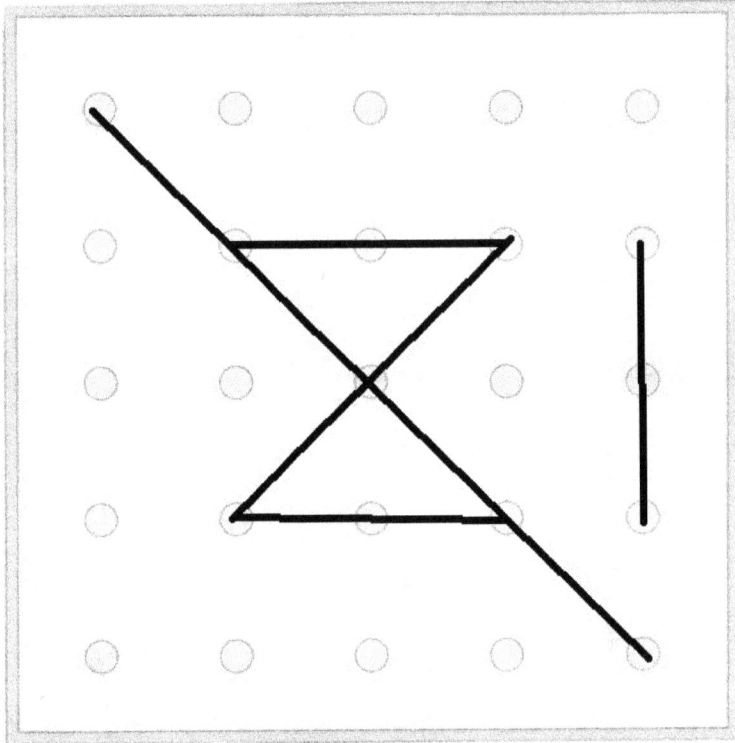

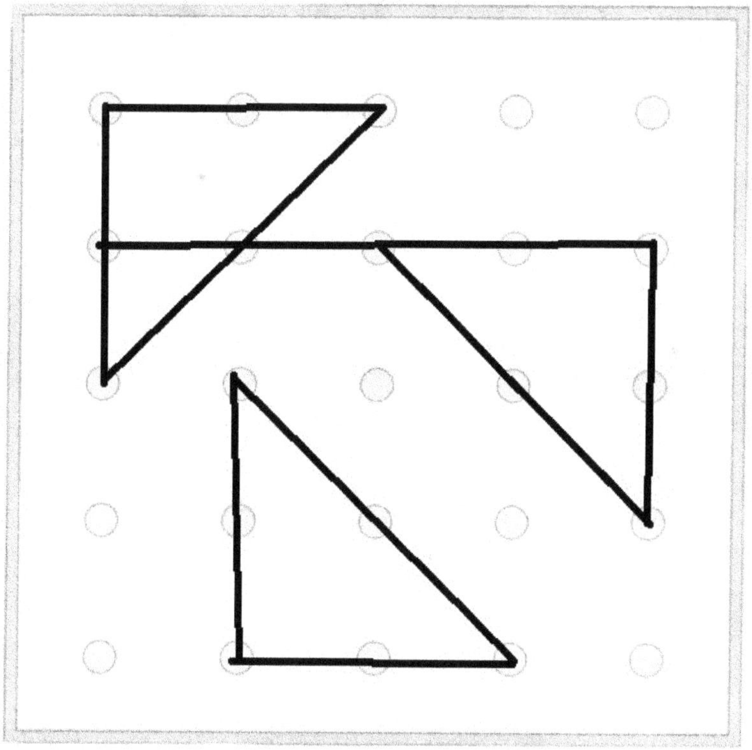

LEVEL 4

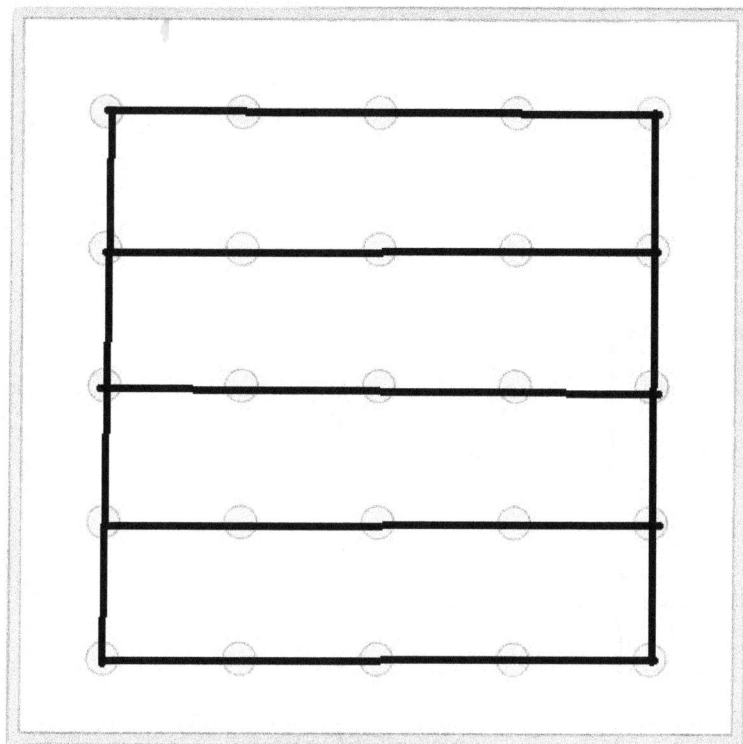

1) How many rubber bands will you need to complete this challenge? ; 2) Where are you going to start? Then what? Tell me the moves all the way to the finish; 3) Do you think you will be able to complete this design?

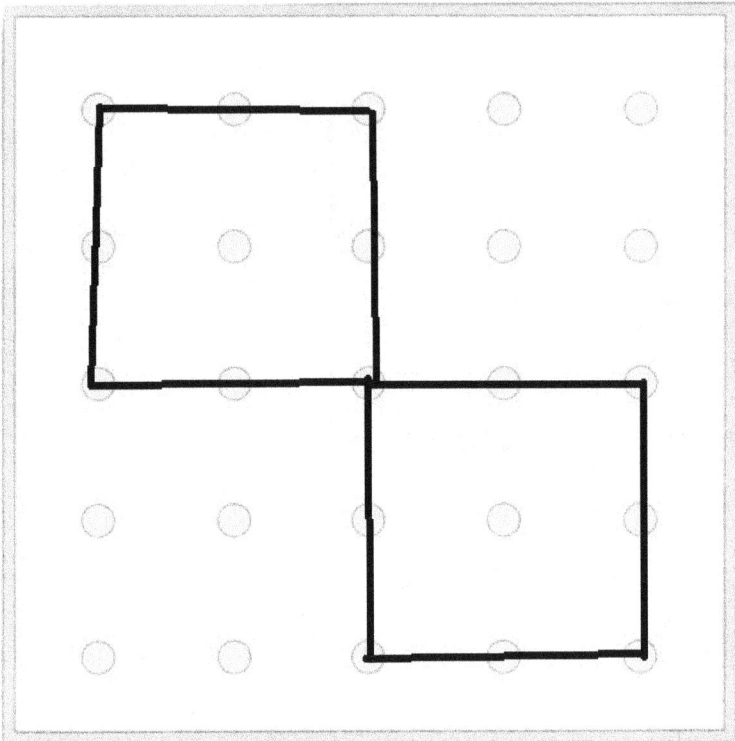

1) How many rubber bands will you need to complete this challenge? ; 2) Where are you going to start? Then what? Tell me the moves all the way to the finish 3) Do you think you will be able to complete this design?"

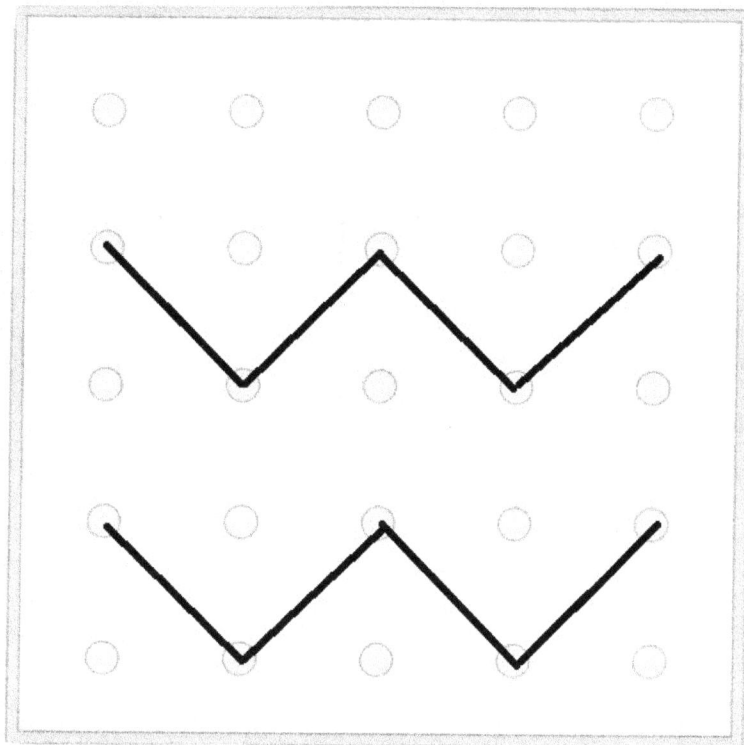

1) How many rubber bands will you need to complete this challenge? ; 2) Where are you going to start? Then what? Tell me the moves all the way to the finish; 3) Do you think you will be able to complete this design?

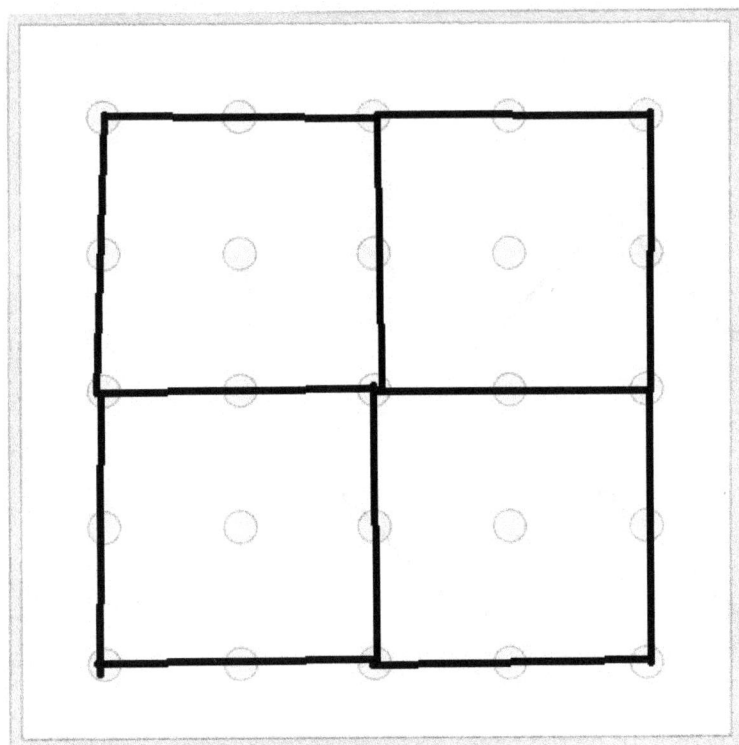

1) How many rubber bands will you need to complete this challenge? ; 2) Where are you going to start? Then what? Tell me the moves all the way to the finish; 3) Do you think you will be able to complete this design?

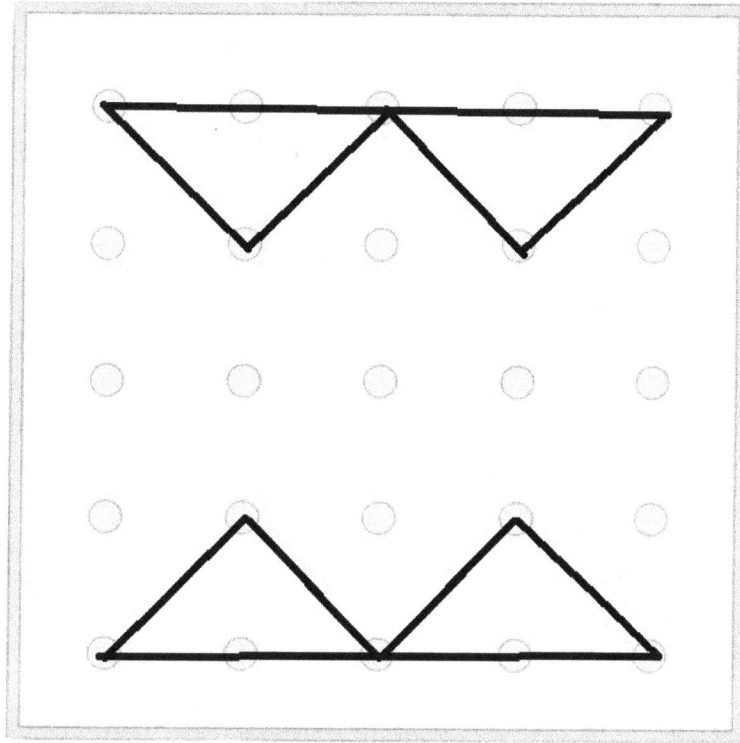

1) How many rubber bands will you need to complete this challenge? ; 2) Where are you going to start? Then what? Tell me the moves all the way to the finish 3) Do you think you will be able to complete this design?"

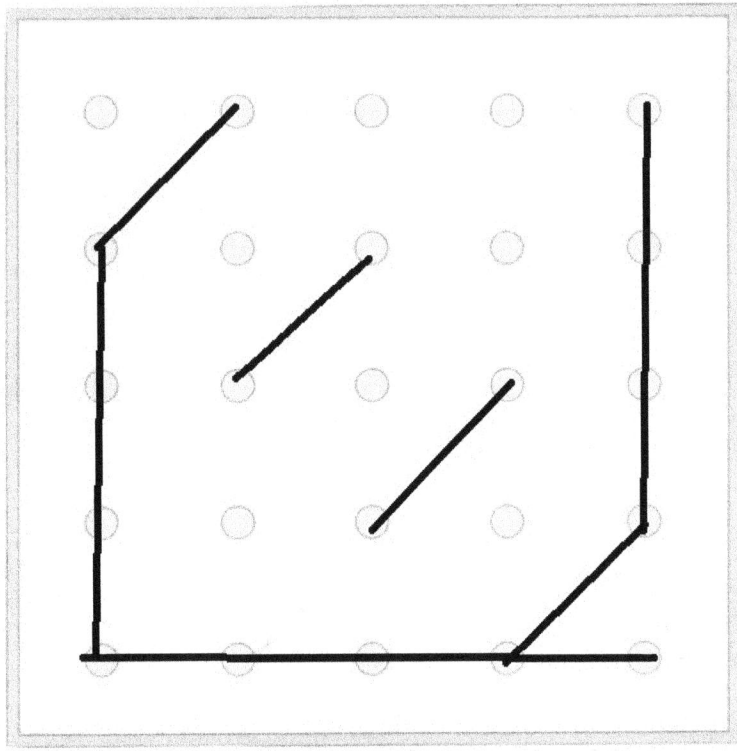

How many rubber bands will you need to complete this challenge? ...OK. Next, where are you going to start? ...And then what? Tell me the moves all the way to the finish. Finally, do you think you will be able to complete this design?"

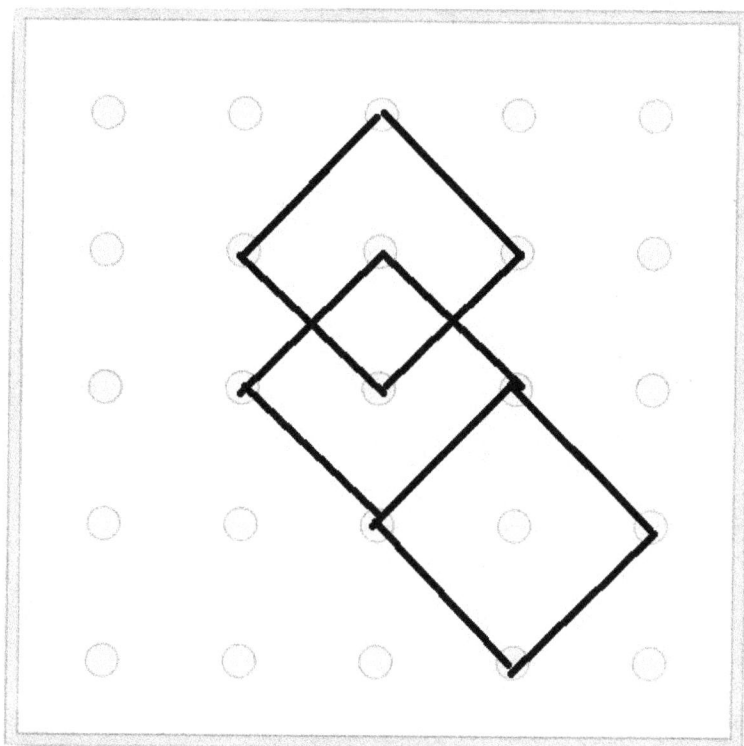

1) How many rubber bands will you need to complete this challenge? ; 2) Where are you going to start? Then what? Tell me the moves all the way to the finish 3) Do you think you will be able to complete this design?"

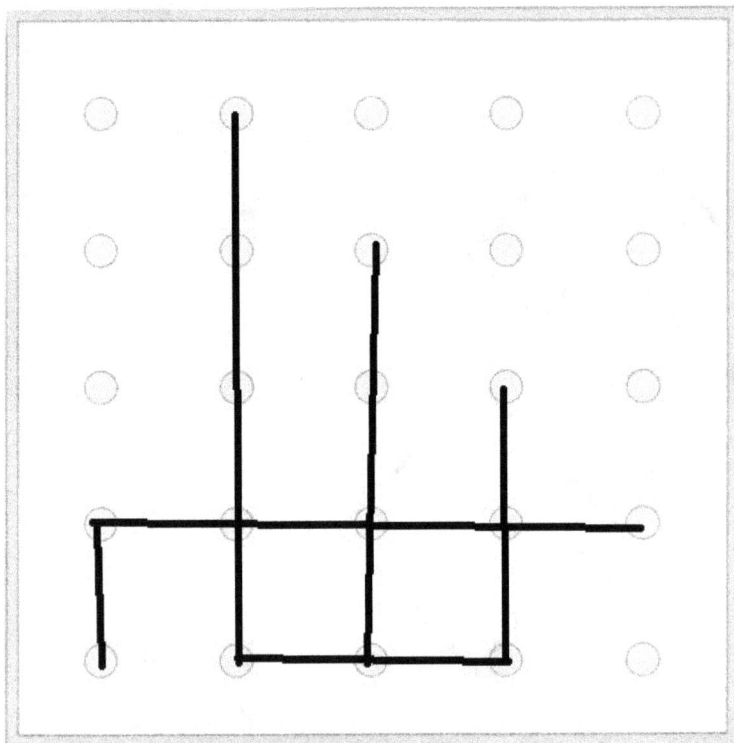

1) How many rubber bands will you need to complete this challenge? ; 2) Where are you going to start? Then what? Tell me the moves all the way to the finish ; 3) Do you think you will be able to complete this design?"

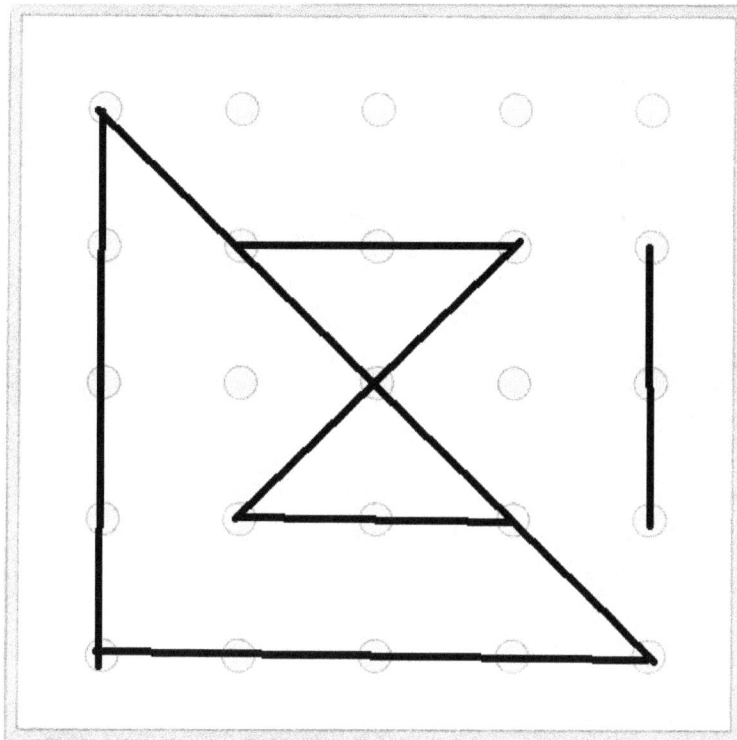

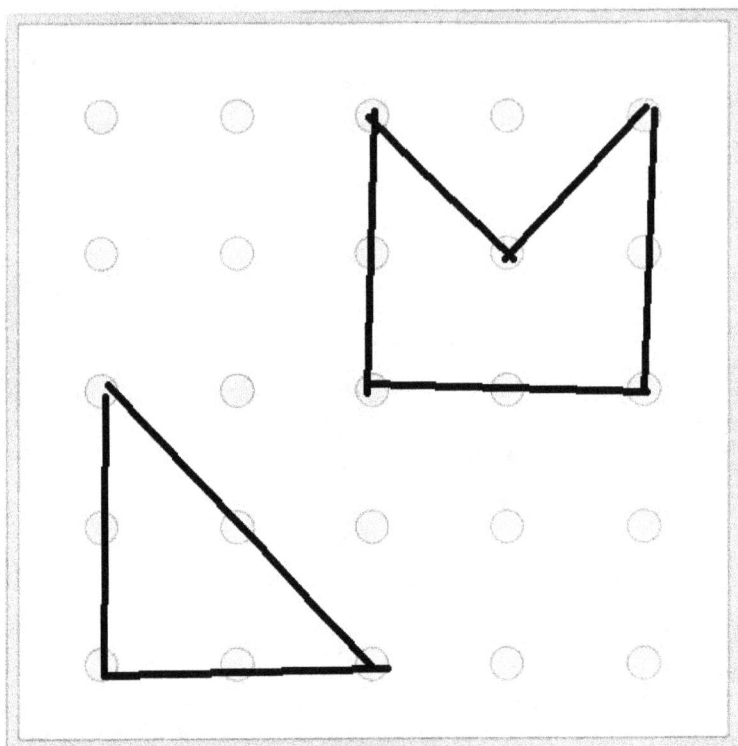

1) How many rubber bands will you need to complete this challenge? ; 2) Where are you going to start? Then what? Tell me the moves all the way to the finish 3) Do you think you will be able to complete this design?"

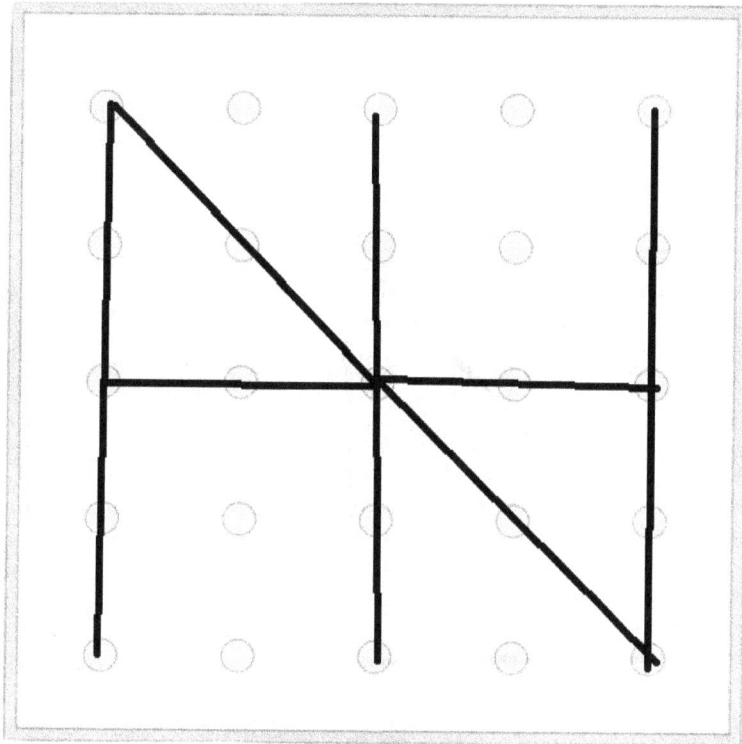

1) How many rubber bands will you need to complete this challenge? ; 2) Where are you going to start? Then what? Tell me the moves all the way to the finish 3) Do you think you will be able to complete this design?"

1) How many rubber bands will you need to complete this challenge? ; 2) Where are you going to start? Then what? Tell me the moves all the way to the finish; 3) Do you think you will be able to complete this design?

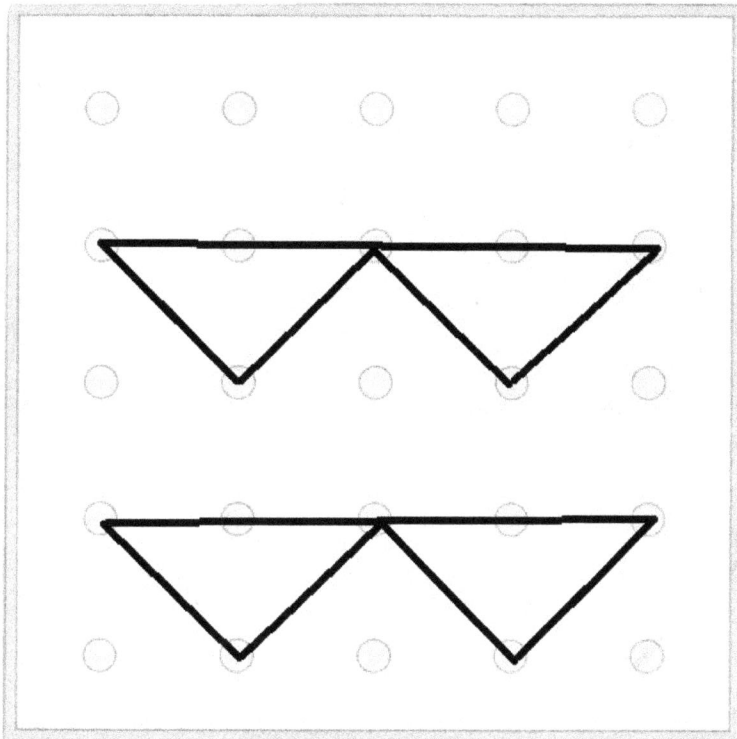

1) How many rubber bands will you need to complete this challenge? ; 2) Where are you going to start? Then what? Tell me the moves all the way to the finish; 3) Do you think you will be able to complete this design?

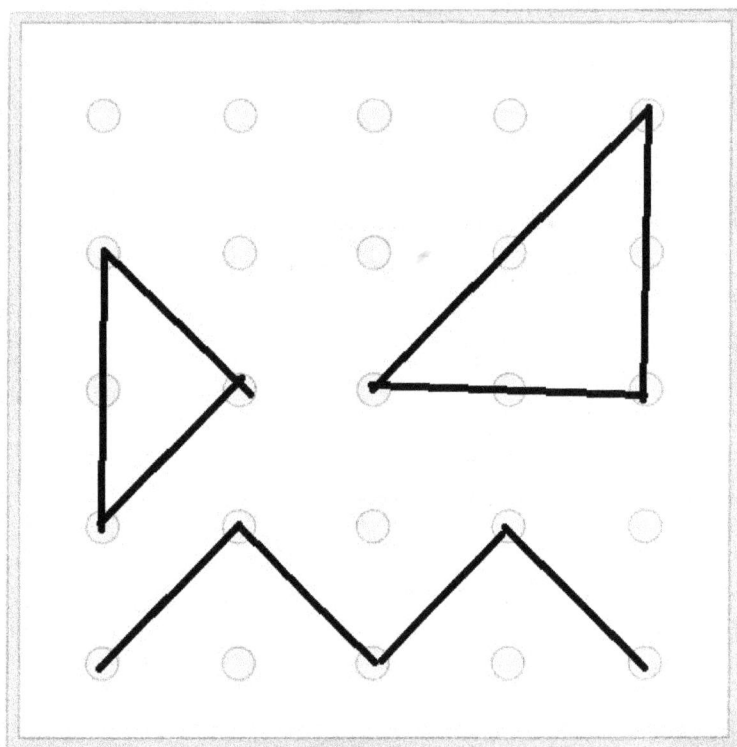

1) How many rubber bands will you need to complete this challenge? ; 2) Where are you going to start? Then what? Tell me the moves all the way to the finish; 3) Do you think you will be able to complete this design?

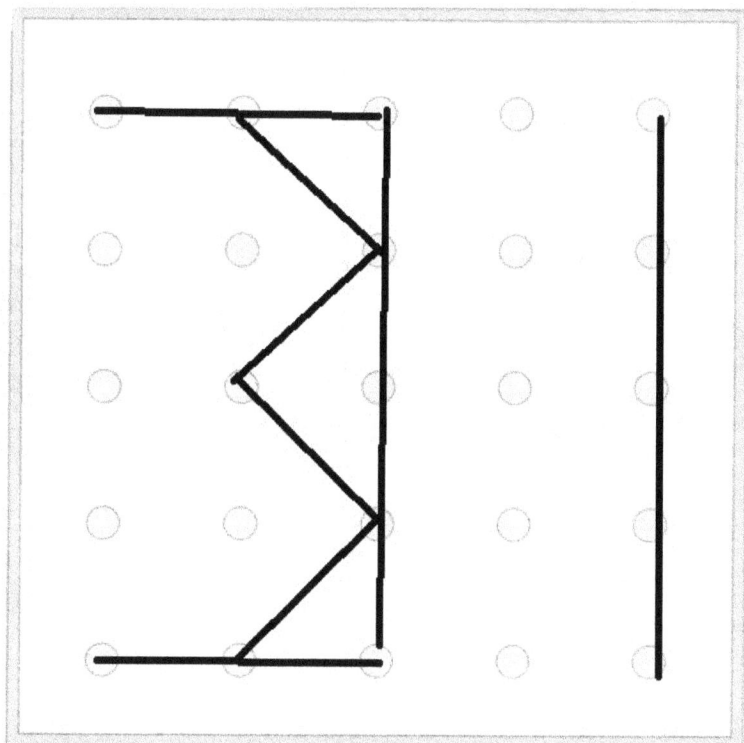

1) How many rubber bands will you need to complete this challenge? ; 2) Where are you going to start? Then what? Tell me the moves all the way to the finish; 3) Do you think you will be able to complete this design?

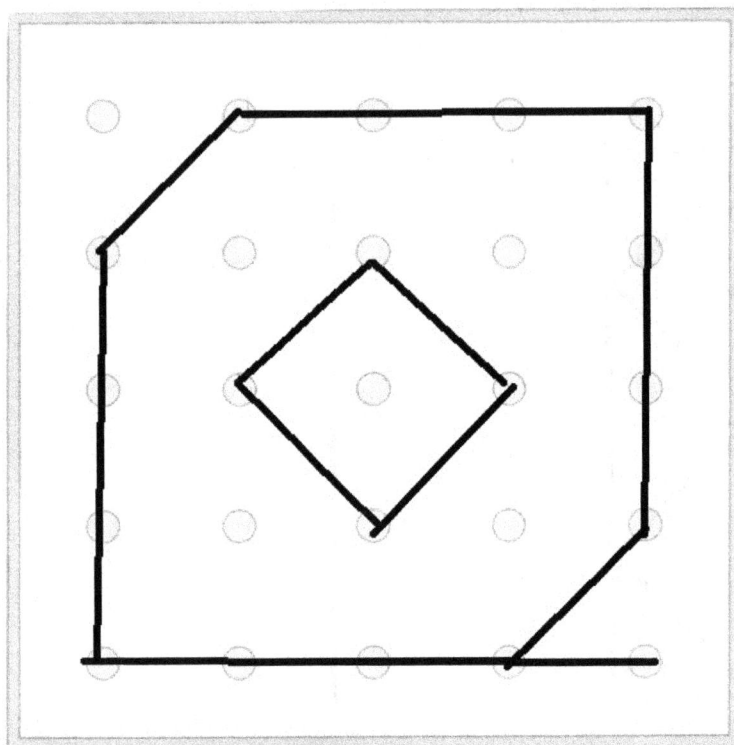

1) How many rubber bands will you need to complete this challenge? ; 2) Where are you going to start? Then what? Tell me the moves all the way to the finish; 3) Do you think you will be able to complete this design?

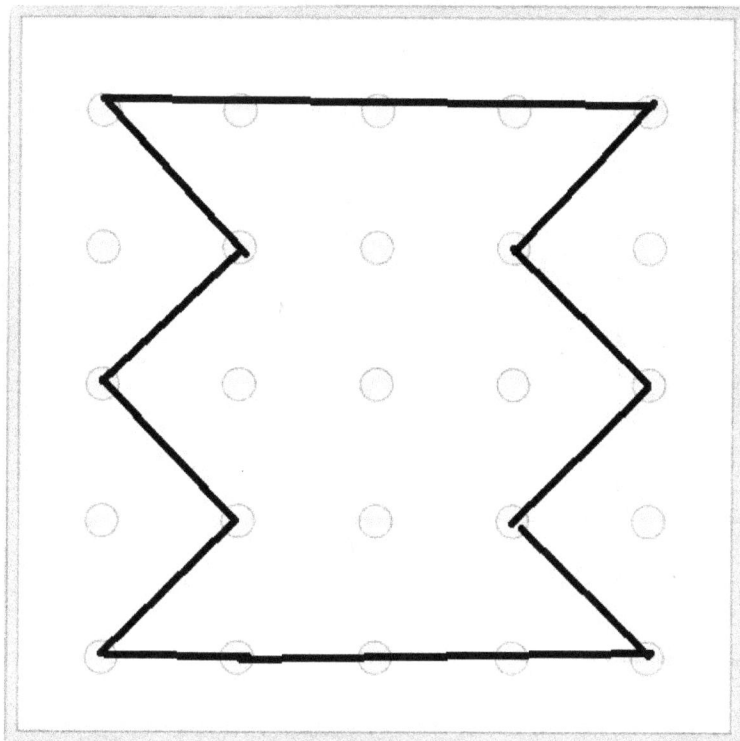

1) How many rubber bands will you need to complete this challenge? ; 2) Where are you going to start? Then what? Tell me the moves all the way to the finish; 3) Do you think you will be able to complete this design?

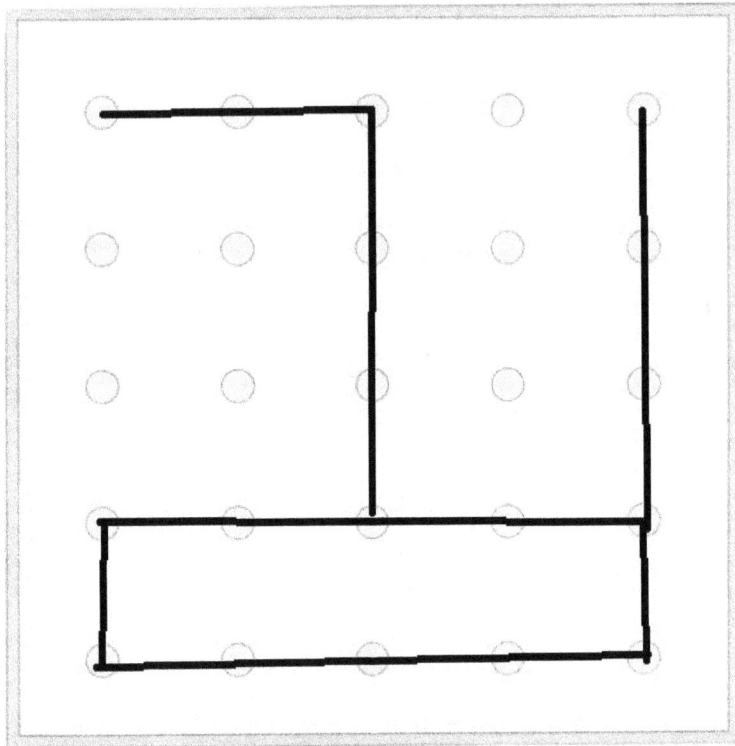

1) How many rubber bands will you need to complete this challenge? ; 2) Where are you going to start? Then what? Tell me the moves all the way to the finish; 3) Do you think you will be able to complete this design?

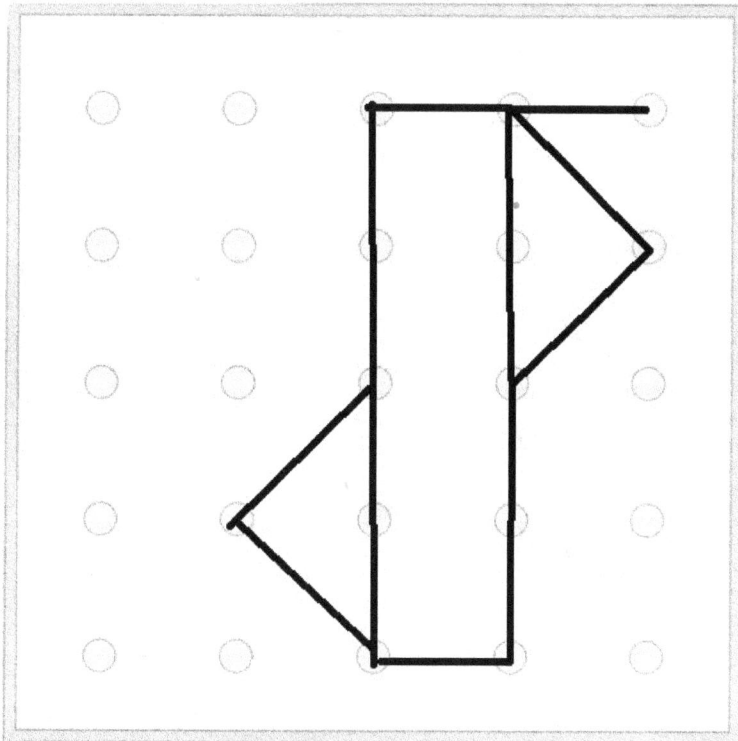

YEAH!!!!!

YOU FINISHED LEVEL 4 !!!

You are getting this!

LEVEL 5

1) How many rubber bands will you need to complete this challenge? ; 2) Where are you going to start? Then what? Tell me the moves all the way to the finish; 3) Do you think you will be able to complete this design?

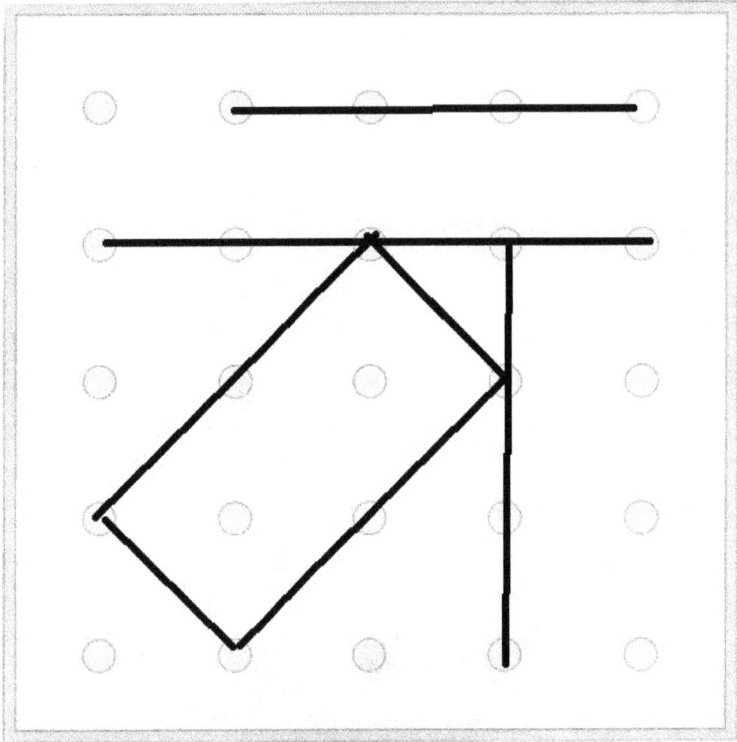

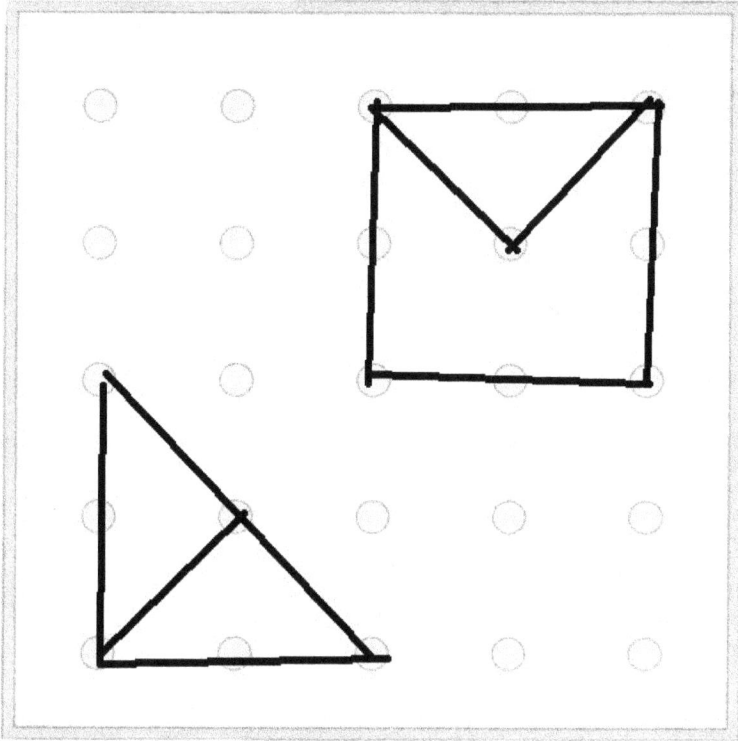

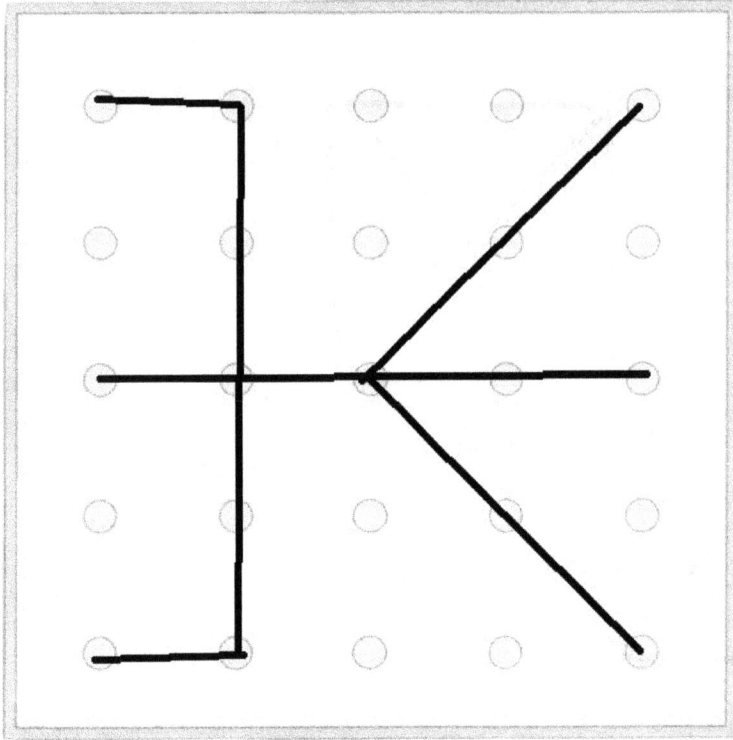

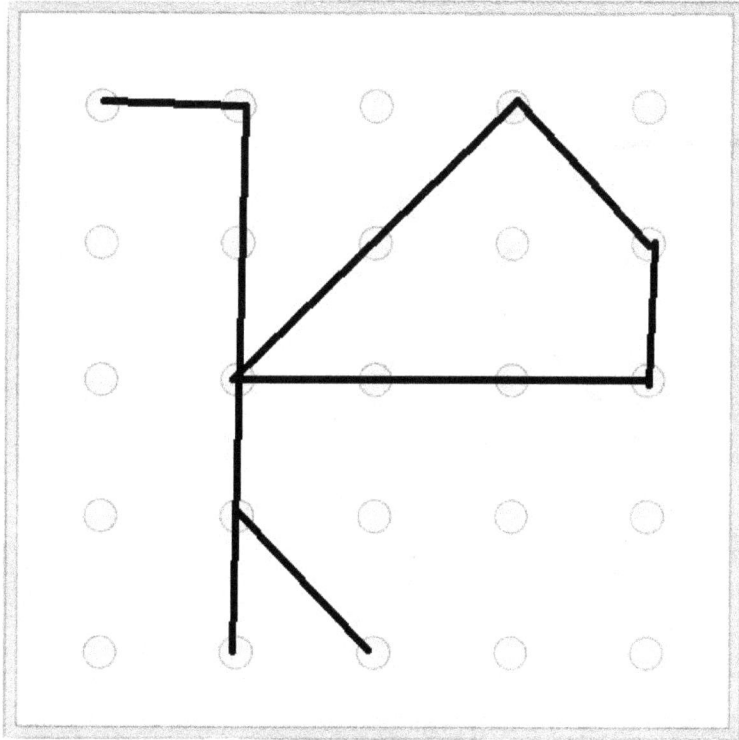

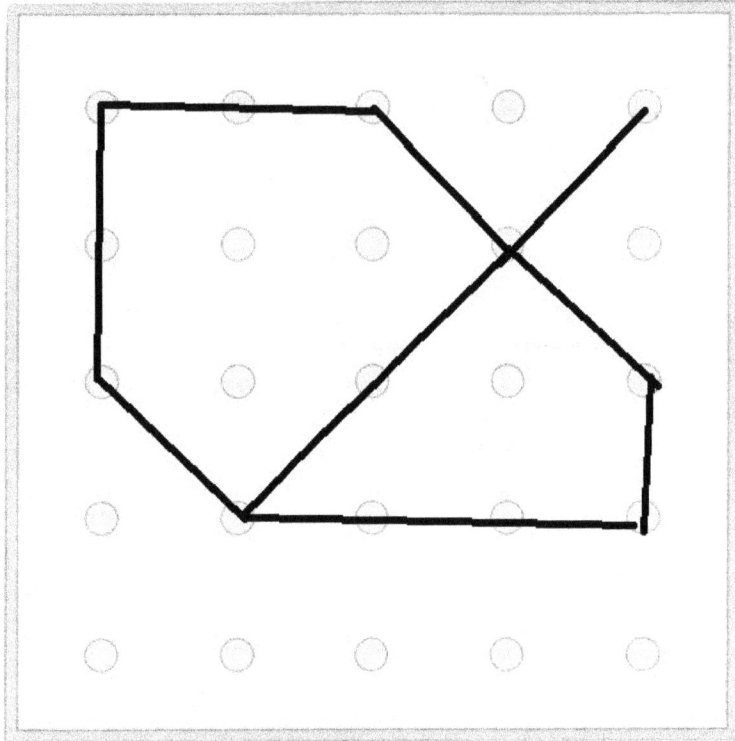

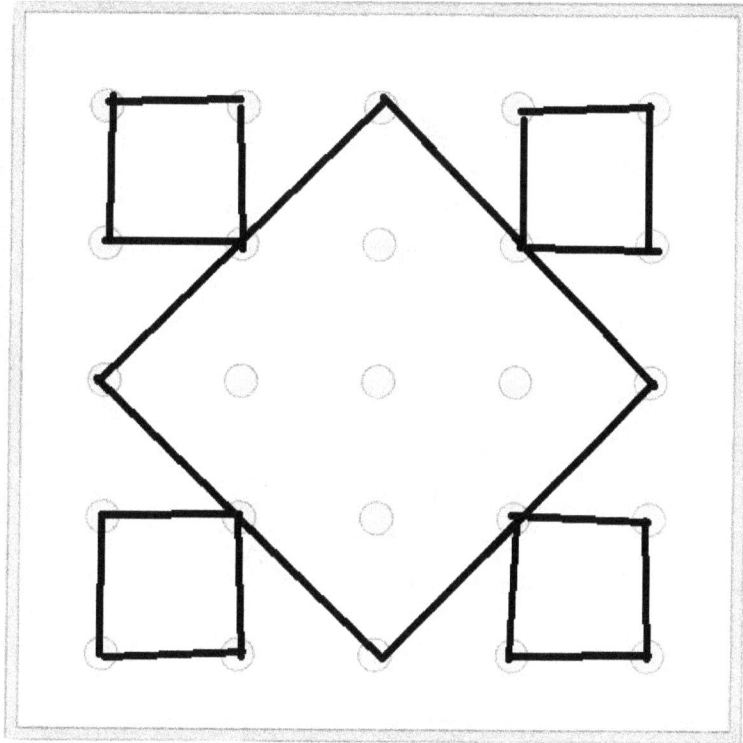

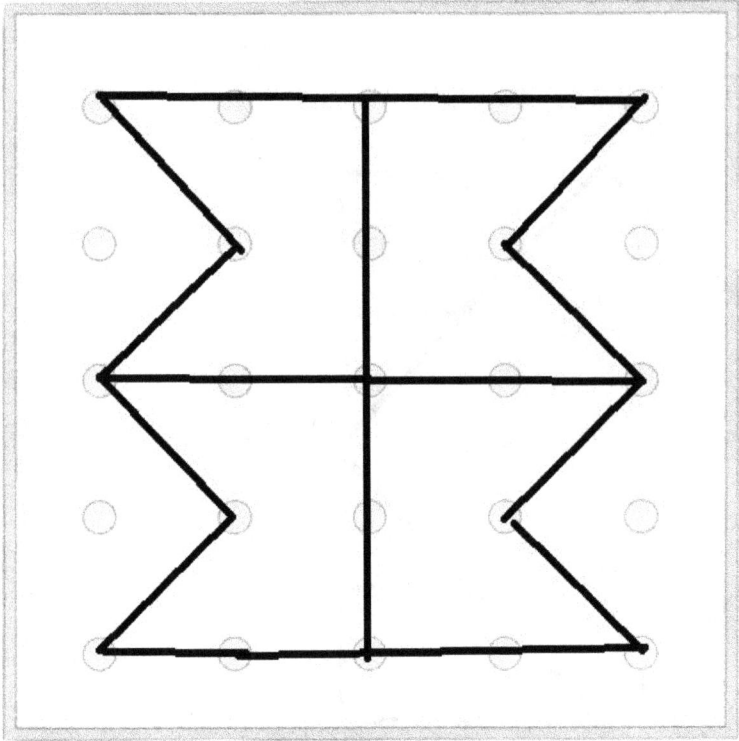

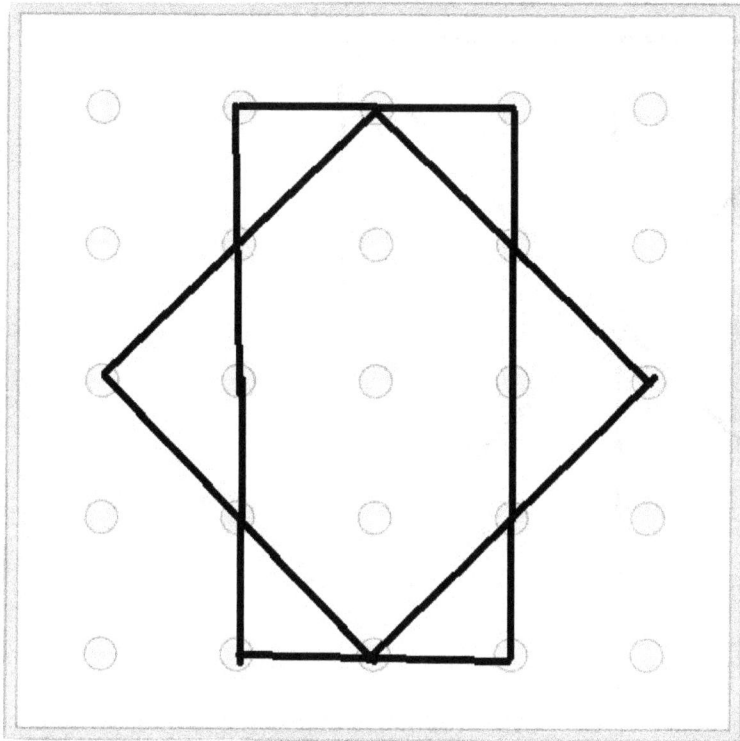

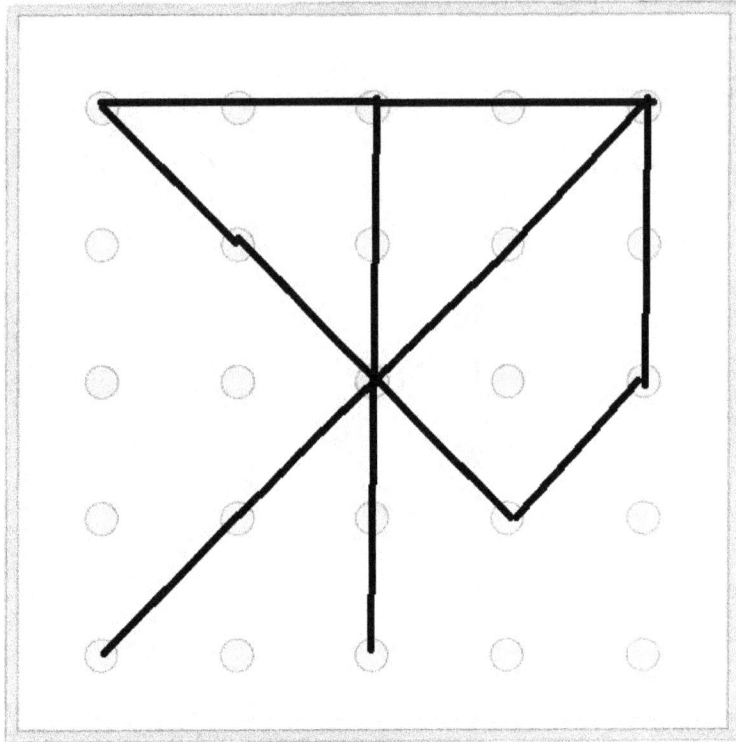

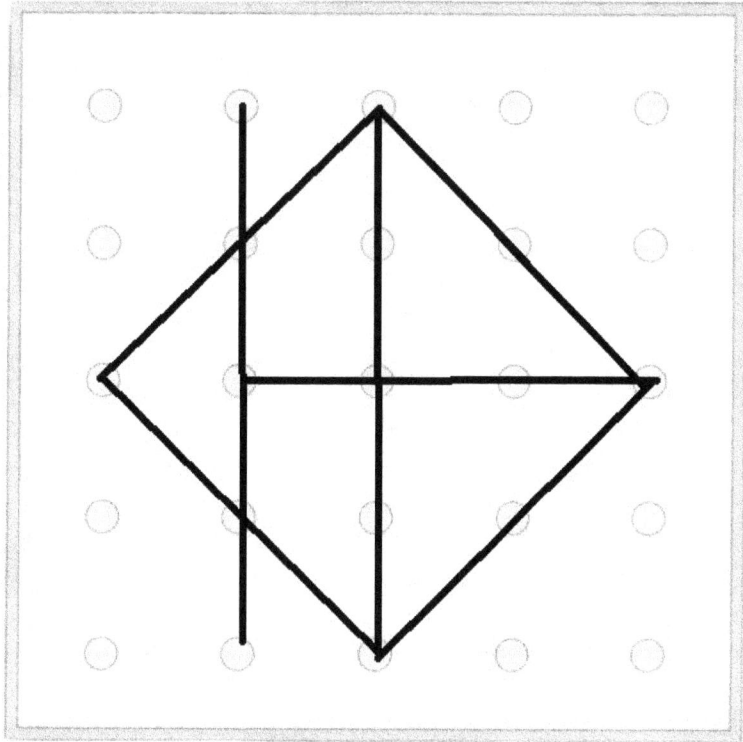

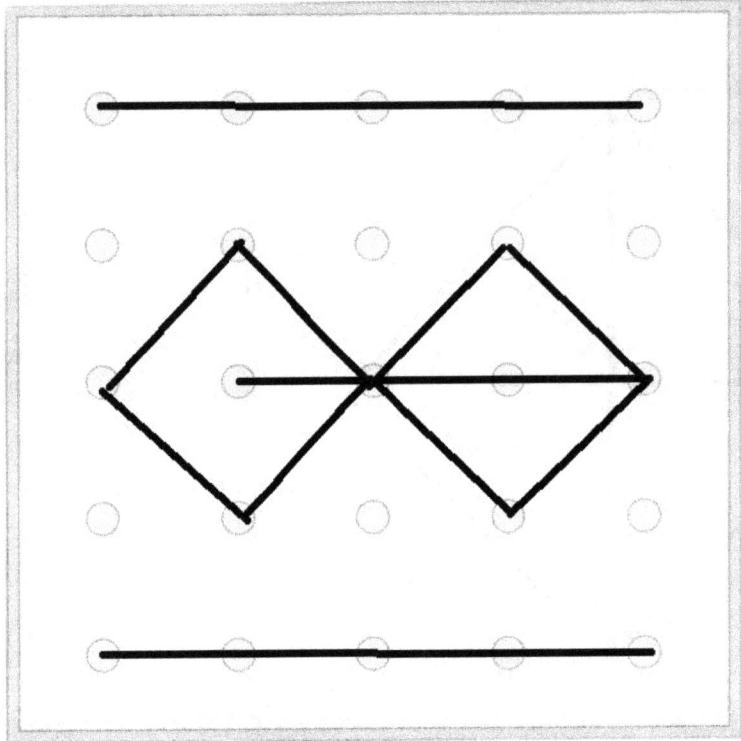

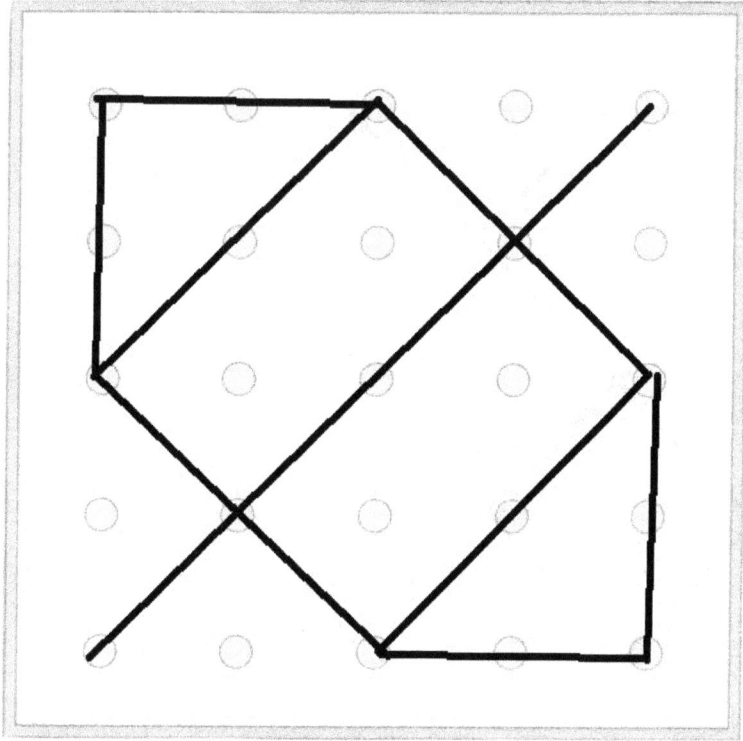

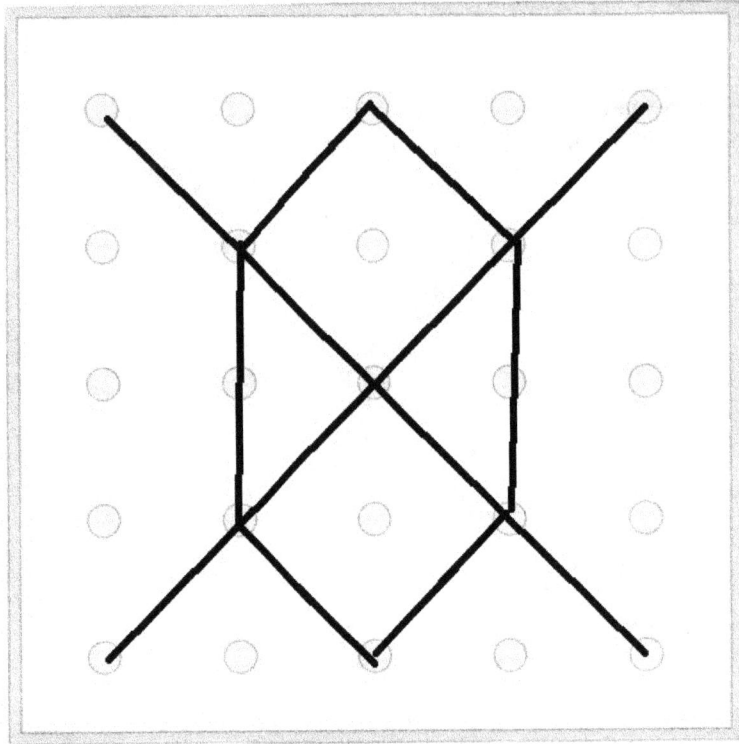

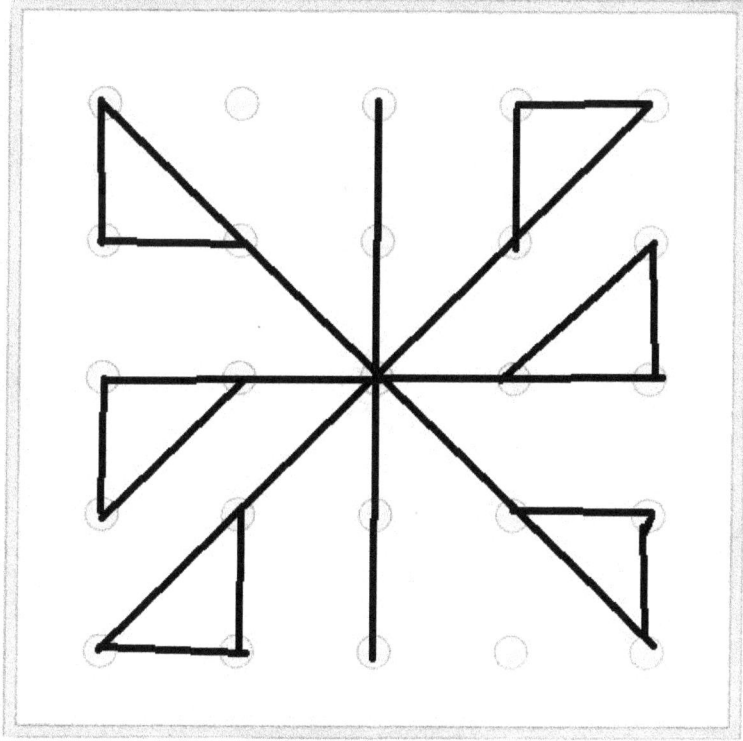

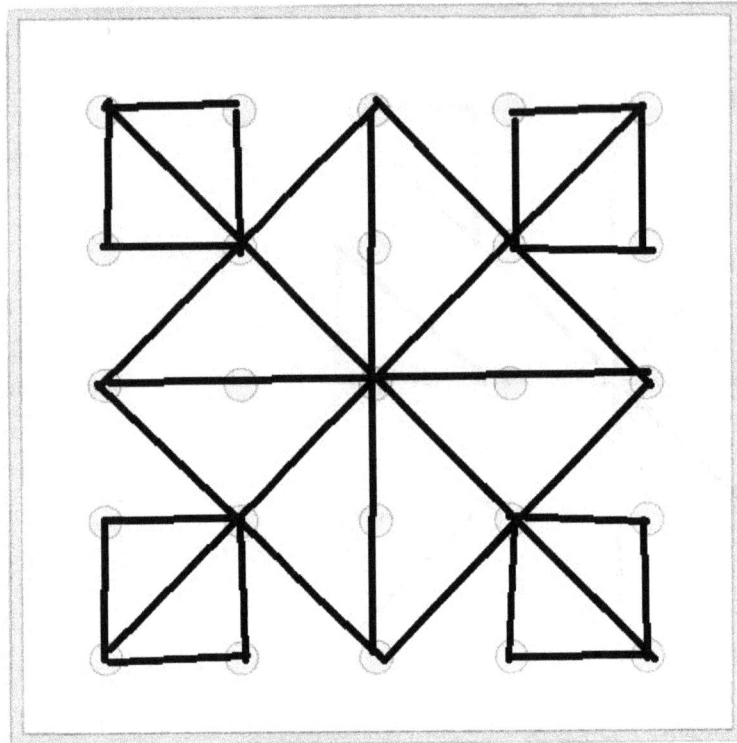

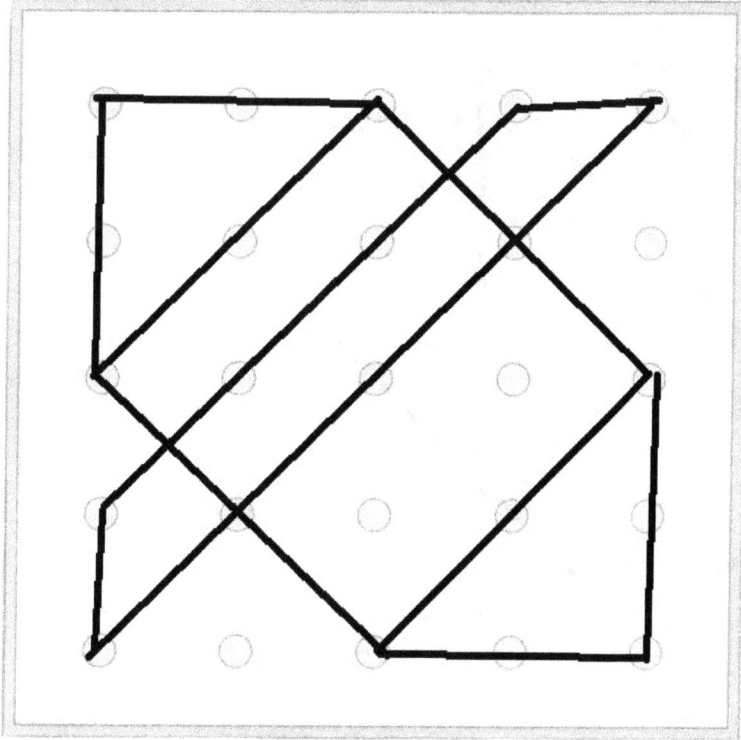

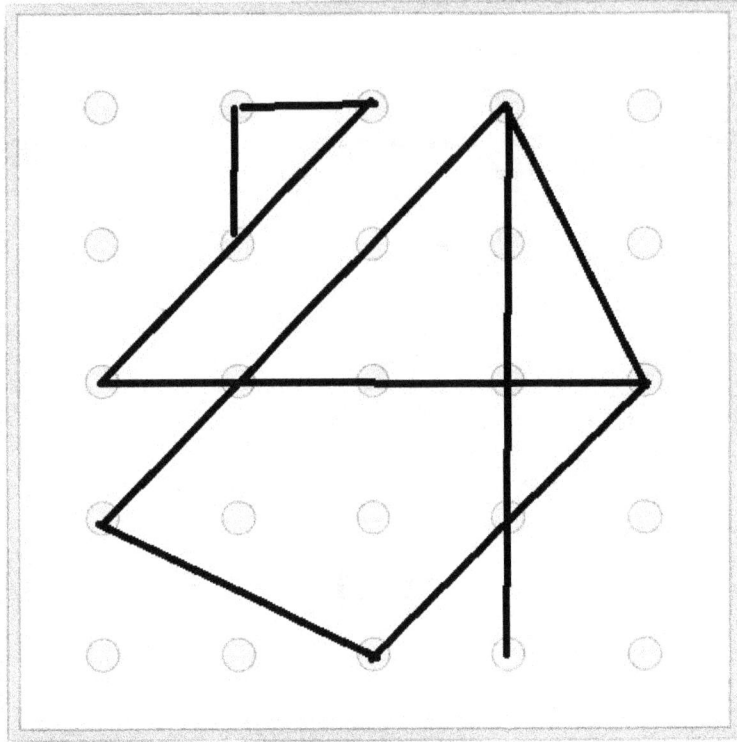

OUTSTANDING!!!!
YOU COMPLETED LEVEL 5

LEVEL 6

125

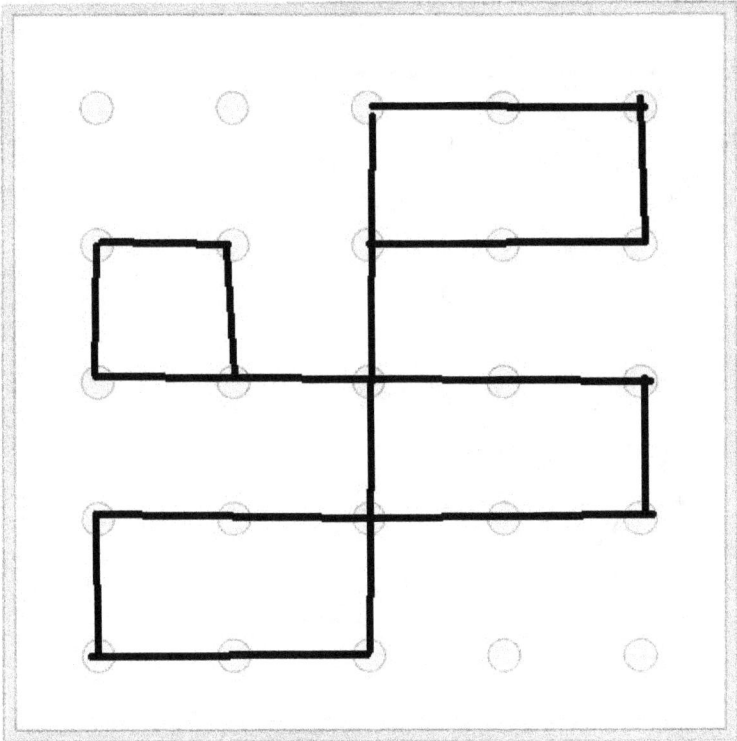

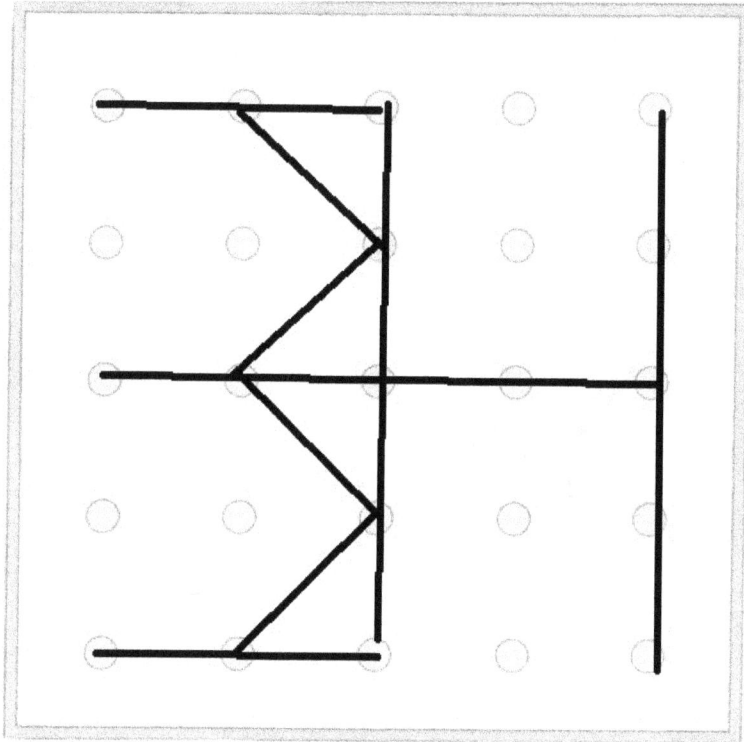

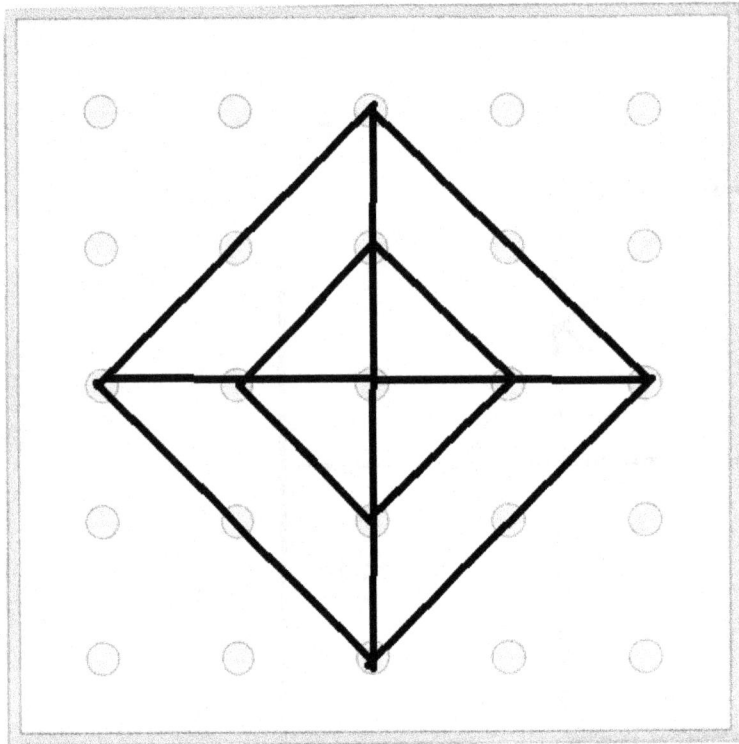

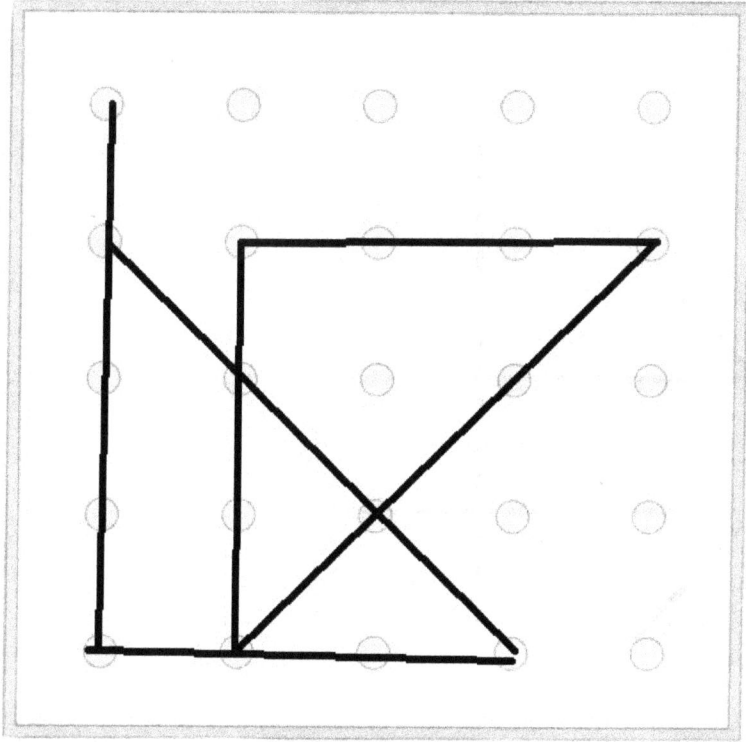

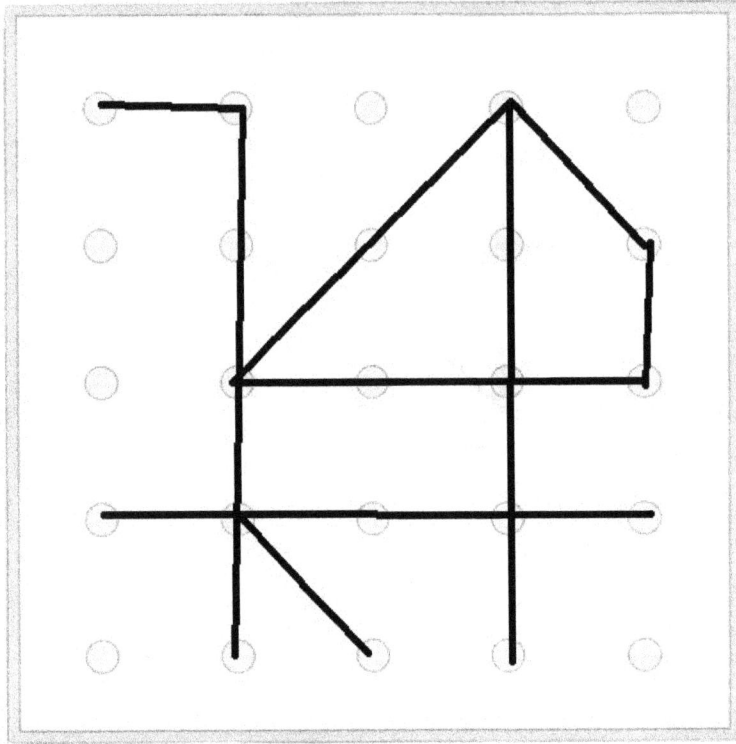

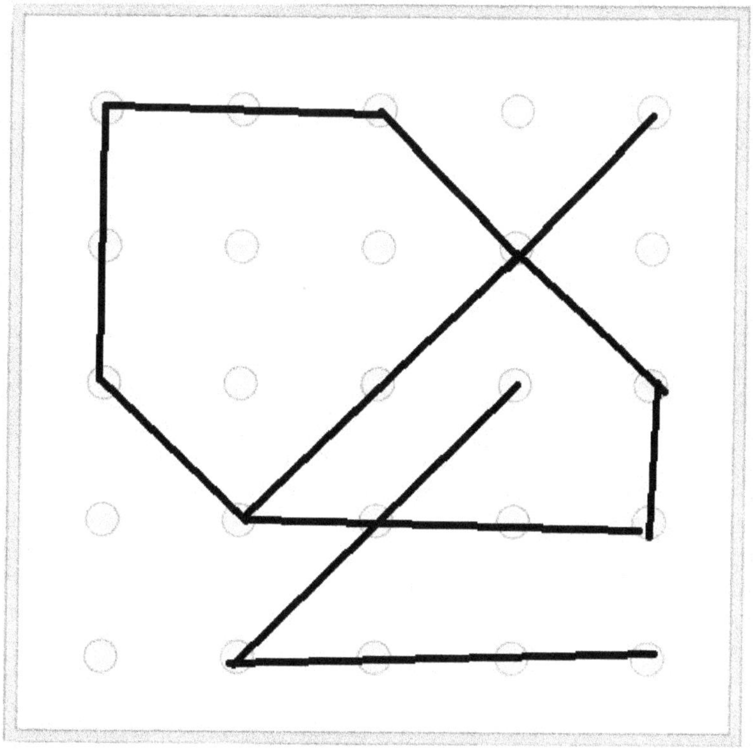

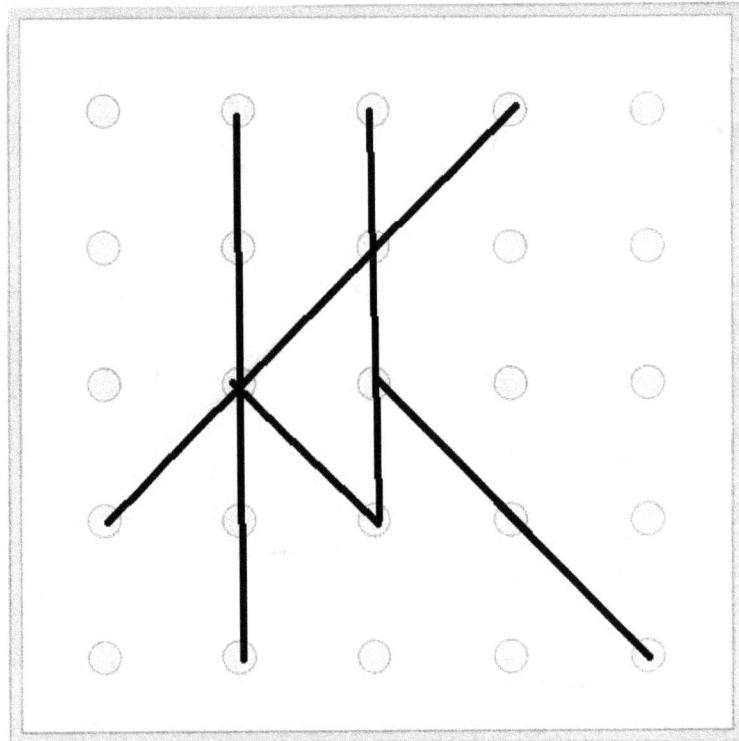

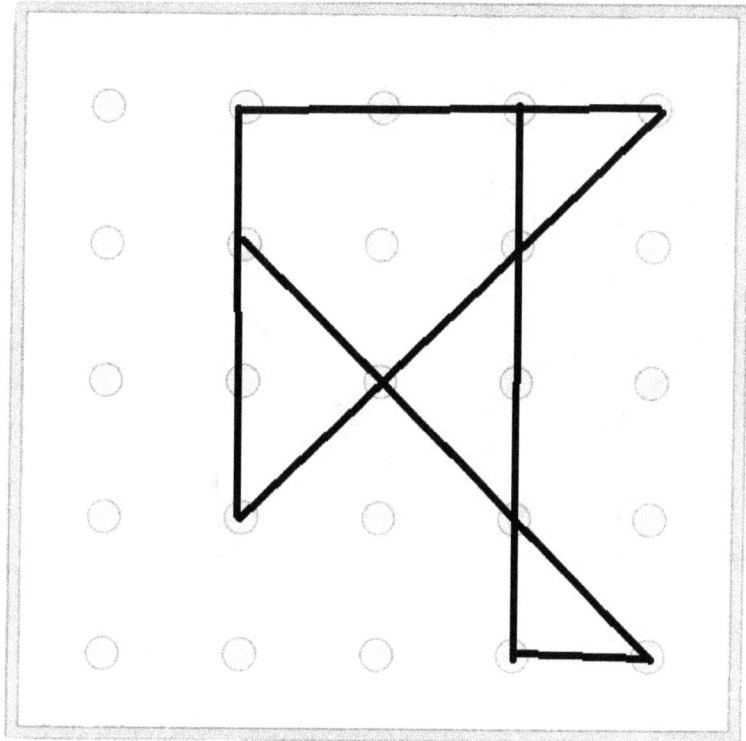

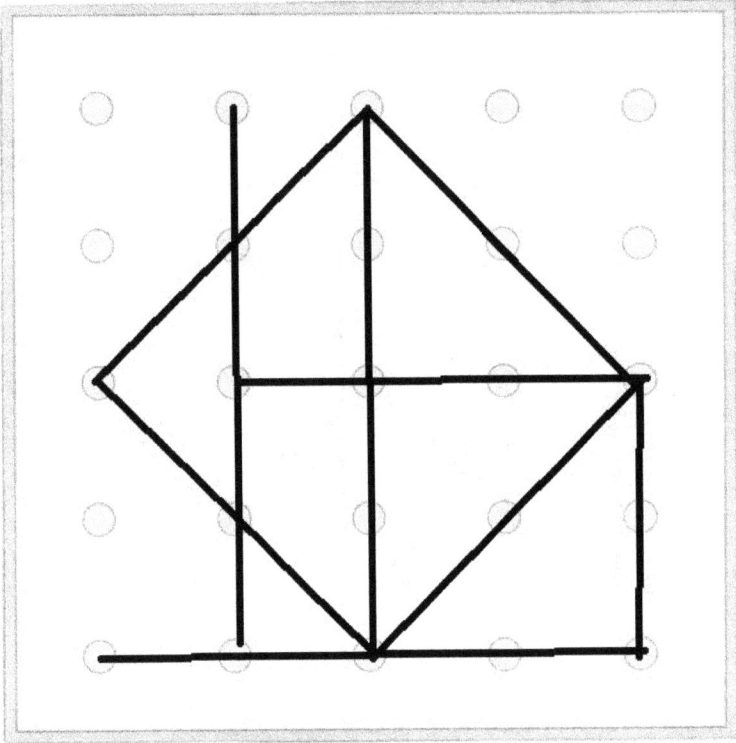

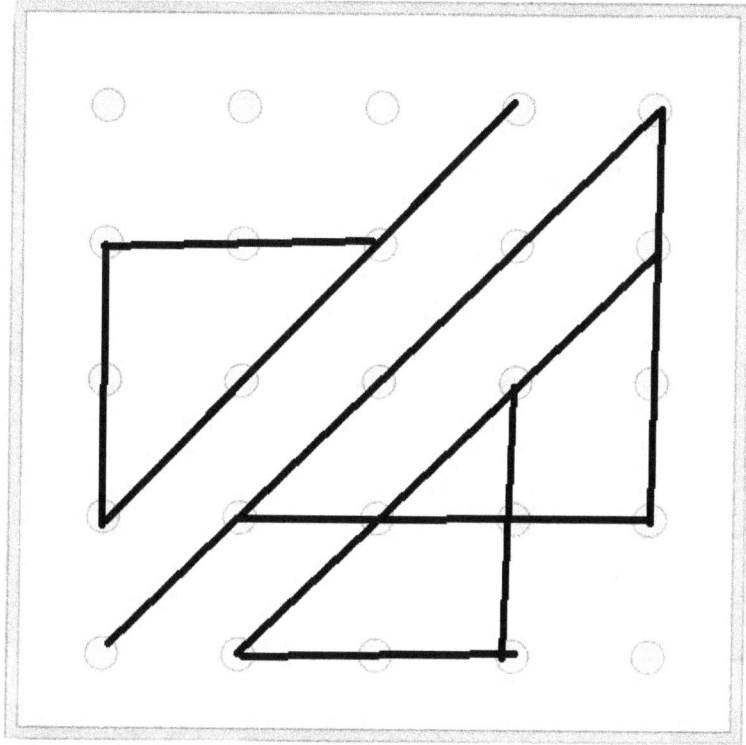

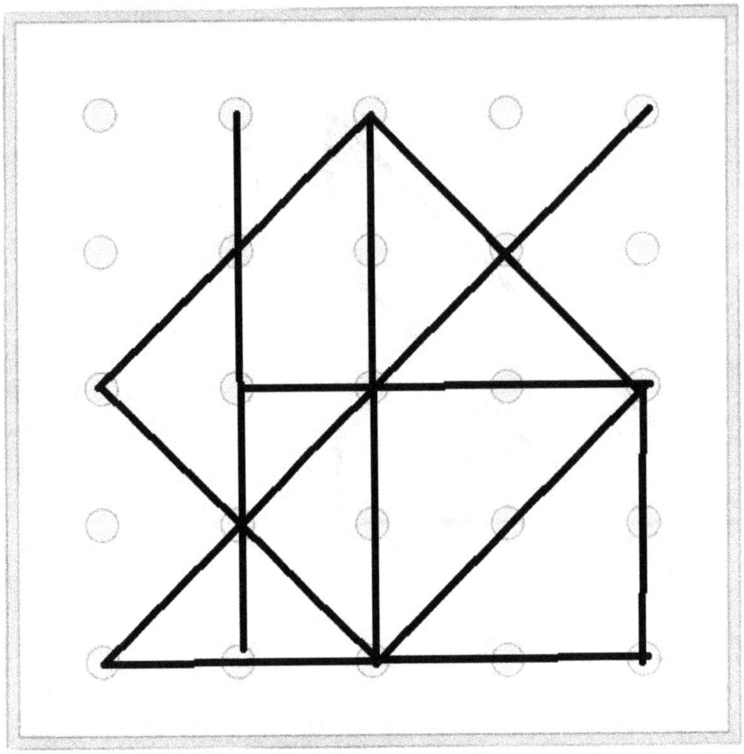

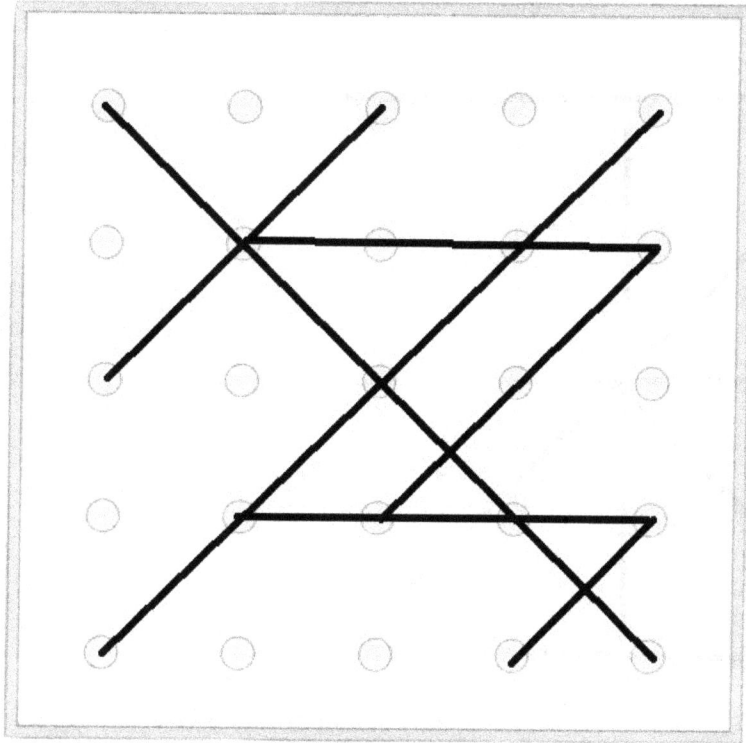

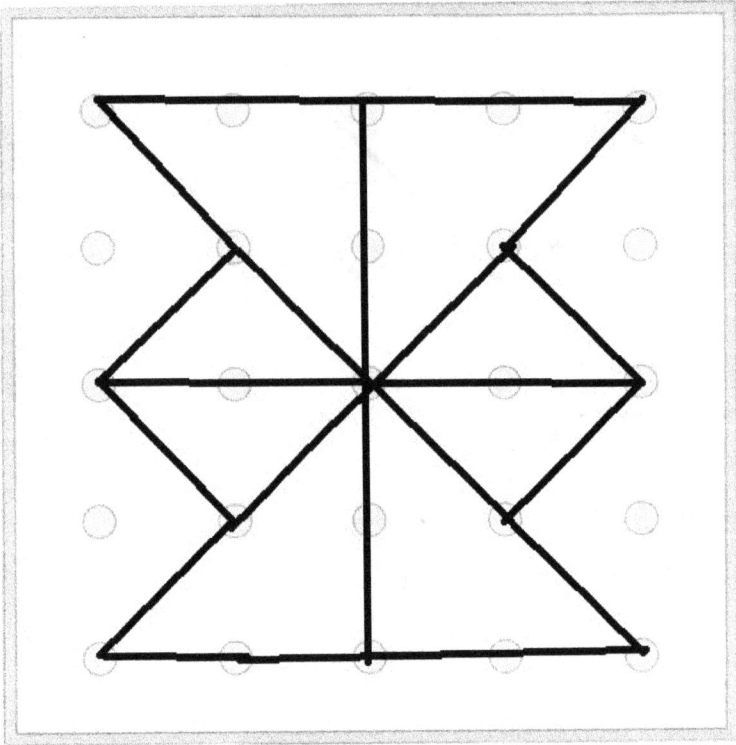

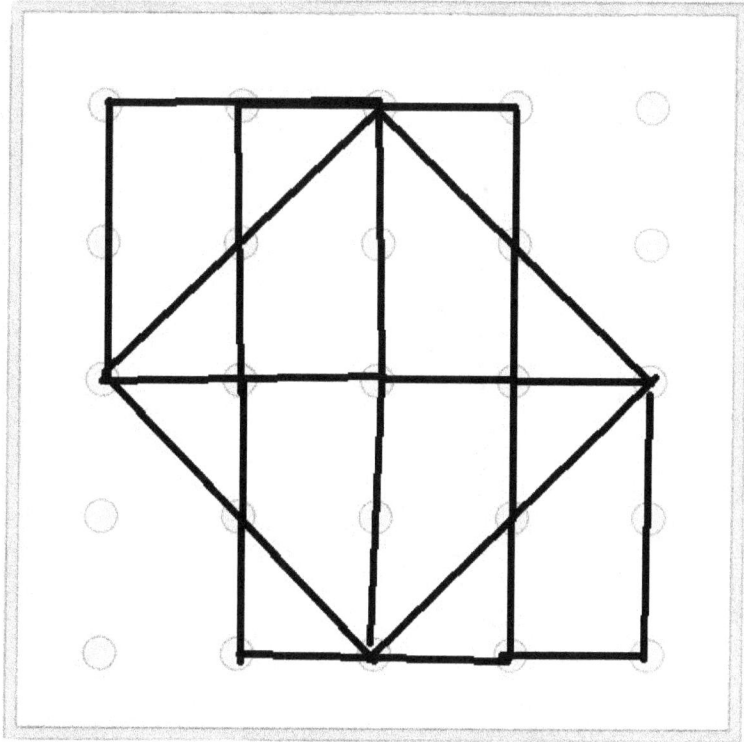

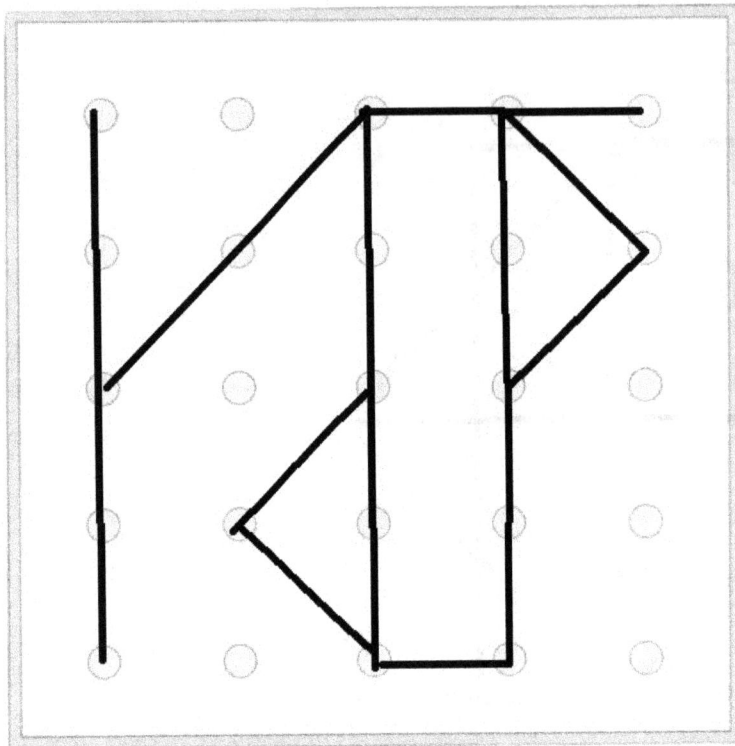

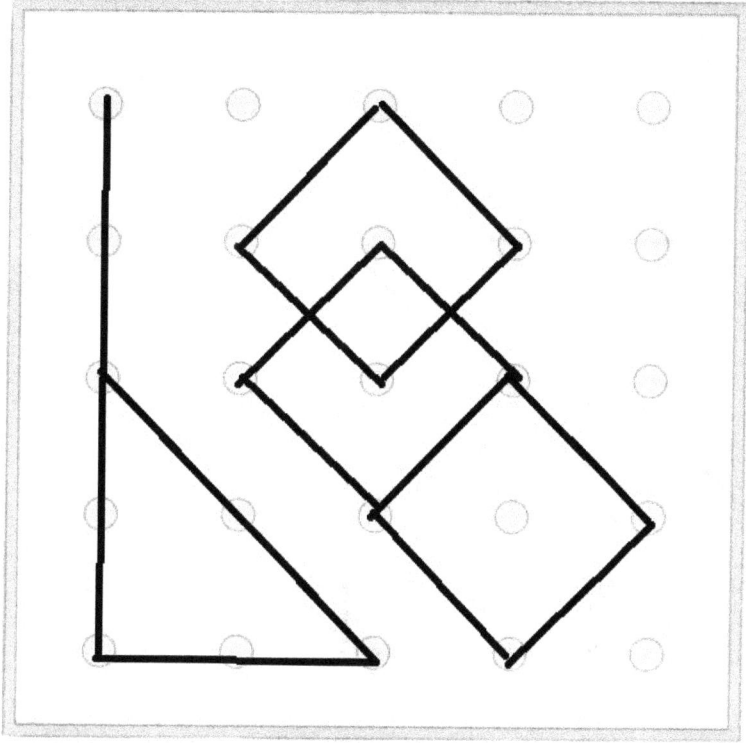

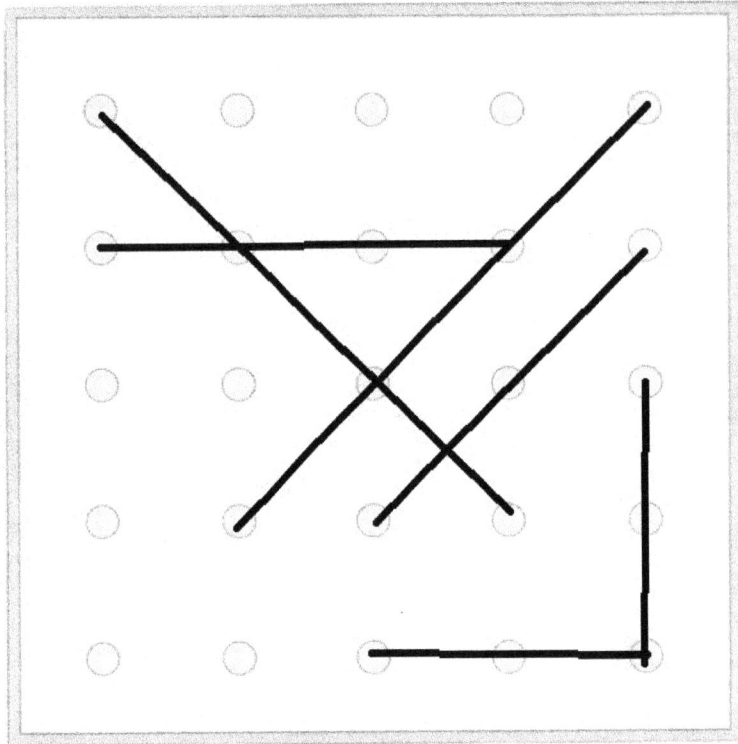

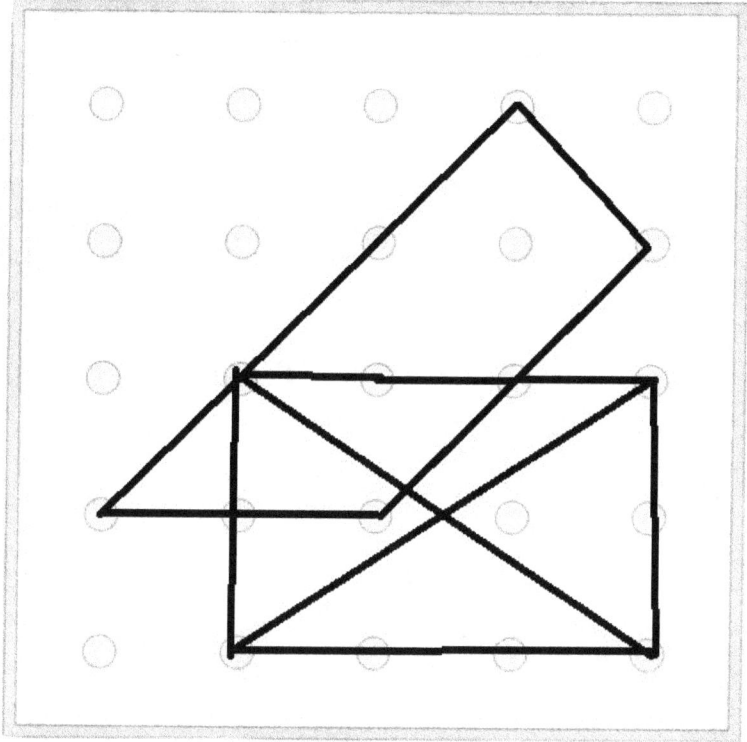

YOU FINISHED LEVEL 6 AND THIS PROGRAM!

YOU ARE AN AWESOME THINKER!!!

www.ingramcontent.com/pod-product-compliance
Lightning Source LLC
Chambersburg PA
CBHW081647270326
41933CB00018B/3373